The Greatest Guide to

Winning
Competiti

This is a **GREATEST**GUIDES title

Greatest Guides Limited, Woodstock, Bridge End, Warwick CV34 6PD, United Kingdom

www.greatestguides.com

Series created by Harshad Kotecha

Greatest Guides is committed to a sustainable future for our planet. This book is printed on paper certified by the Forest Stewardship Council.

Printed and bound in the United Kingdom

ISBN 978-1-907906-04-6

For my family and good friends who have celebrated my prize-winning success and have willingly shared the rewards.

Contents

Foreword by Vivienne Elsworth

When Karen told me she was planning to write a book which revealed her competition winning techniques, I thought she was joking, mainly because it's not in her best interests to do so. I had no hesitation in writing this foreword though as, after all, we have been sharing our prize winnings for more years than I care to remember!

Our first head-to-head contest occurred in 1992 when we found ourselves competing for the same scientific job vacancy for a major healthcare research facility. Fortunately we were both offered a job and we have been friends ever since.

It soon became obvious, however, that we had a lot more in common – we were both competition enthusiasts. Karen had taken a few years' break from entering competitions but it didn't take very much persuasion from me to get her back on track and entering competitions again. Before long, she renewed her enthusiasm and soon secured an awesome reputation in competition circles for winning. I'm pleased to have played a part, albeit a small one, in Karen's 'comping' success story.

Karen is the only person I know who arrives for a girls' night out in a brand new car that she has just won (using less than ten words on a piece of paper) or who sends a postcard from a holiday that she has won (thanking me for the entry form!). Our hobby is a source of great enjoyment to us both.

Karen has maintained her winning streak and further improved her own highly-successful techniques. Her prize list is impressive and ever-expanding. I trust that you will find her book of tips inspiring, informative and rewarding.

Happy comping!

Vivienne Elsworth
Friend and fellow comper

A few words from Karen …

Congratulations! You are already on the road to becoming a successful prize winner.

During my experience of being a highly successful 'comper' (a term commonly used to describe a competition enthusiast), I have developed and perfected my own techniques that win prizes time and time again. The phenomenal array of prizes that I have gained from entering consumer competitions ranges from cars, cash and holidays, to household items and meals out in exclusive restaurants; many are experiences that simply cannot be bought. Soon, this success could be yours too.

After constant suggestion from family and friends I have succumbed to sharing the secrets of my lucrative hobby with you, and have outlined how I have consistently and considerably improved my chances of winning virtually any prize I desire. I hope you enjoy as much success and pleasure from this hobby as I do at the moment, and that it lasts a lifetime.

There might be a few friends and family members who are predisposed to mock competitions and their entrants, believing that prizes are 'pre-assigned' or 'fixed'; I'm sure you've heard of this. Don't worry – your first big win will remedy the problem.

I have been a very successful competition winner for most of my life. My competitive streak developed as a very young child, when I accidentally hit on a technique which enabled me to regularly win the majority of the local coloring competitions. I was ruthless in my determination to win in those early years, and still am. At present, I focus primarily on writing slogans (also known as tie-breakers) and submitting postcard entries – these formats lend themselves perfectly to the psychological manipulation techniques that you will encounter in this book.

I wish you much success and enjoyment with your new hobby.

Happy comping!

Karen

Getting Started

"Winning isn't everything… it's the only thing."

Vincent van Gough

Chapter 1
Getting Started

Engaging in a new pursuit or hobby is both exciting and daunting. I'm sure we all recognize acquaintances who dabble at something and get nowhere fast, and others who seek advice, join clubs of like-minded people and aim for success; entering competitions is no different. This book will serve as a jargon-buster, whilst also offering you hints and tips to get you started with 'comping', thereby priming you with the knowledge you require to get started on the exciting journey of entering and winning local and national competitions. The choice of becoming a casual or career comper is yours to make, as you wish.

Congratulations, you're a winner!

These four words will soon be familiar to you, as you eagerly open the congratulatory letters that tumble through your letterbox or fill your mailbox. There will be an unexpected outcome to your new hobby – your mailman will soon become your new best friend. He will become the bringer of good news (usually in the form of long white envelopes) and, of course, your much-awaited prize packages. It would be advisable to make arrangements with him (or her) as to where you would like any large prize packages to be left, in the event that you are not home to receive them.

The route to success

You may not yet realize it, but you have just made one of the most rewarding decisions you are likely to make in your quest to become a successful competition winner.

You will learn the effective, yet simple, rules of how you can manipulate the odds of winning many forms of consumer competitions in your favor. The techniques you will encounter in this indispensable guide have been developed and fine-tuned over many years, and will allow you to compete successfully against the seasoned compers like myself. We all have one goal – success!

Motives

There are many motives for taking the first steps to enter a competition; a particular prize may have caught your attention or your imagination, you might desperately need an item that you would otherwise be unable to afford, or perhaps you have a particular talent that you wish to make good use of. One thing for certain is that you will have a lot of fun chasing your dreams and attempting to make them a reality.

PRIZE T!P

It is easy to lose focus when you start out on the prize-winning journey. Think carefully about the type of competition you wish to enter and which prizes you would like to receive. The thrill of the first win will undoubtedly be an exhilarating experience, and one that you will always remember – it will be even more exciting if you win something that you actually want to keep.

Obsession

There is no doubt that this fascinating and lucrative hobby will bring you and your family many years of enjoyment and rewards, though it should come with one warning: once your confidence grows, and you start to win a few high-value prizes, it will become an obsession. There is no known cure for this, though I can assure you that it will be a harmless and pleasurable addiction. You might experience frustration occasionally, as competition promoters often tend to offer prizes as part of their seasonal advertising campaigns; use the lull between these periods to re-discover your family life.

Priceless

I never cease to be amazed at the riches that can be earned for the price of a postage stamp on a postcard, or a few words written on a piece of paper. Very few competitions cost you anything to enter other than perhaps buying the promoter's product as part of your normal weekly shopping (keep your receipts – they might be useful at a later date). It is likely that your only monetary outlay will be the cost of buying a postage stamp; posting five competition entries a week equates to less than the cost of a pint of beer, and is certainly better for your health. Each prize needs a winner, so why shouldn't one be you?

How much time do you need?

To decorate an envelope, apply stickers to a postcard or fill out a coupon will take a few minutes each. Completing crosswords, writing slogans or researching a product can take upward of half an hour. The time required for taking the perfect photograph, painting a picture or writing a poem depends very much on your desire for perfection.

PRIZE T!P

That dream prize you've set your heart on winning is yours for the taking; the exciting part of the process is finding a way to obtain it. Make a list of items or experiences that would really enhance your life – these will become your long-term targets; cross them off your list as you achieve them.

One of my own 'dream items' was a new car, as a gift for my mom. For many years she thought that winners were pre-chosen for the high-value prizes; I was determined to prove her wrong. I entered several slogans (each of less than ten words), to secure my win. Euphoria is the only way to describe the sensation I experienced when the phone rang and I was informed that I was the winner. Don't be put off by today's world economy fears; there are still plenty of high-value prizes on offer as a result of manufacturing and marketing companies' advertising budgets.

On a winning streak – where it all started for me

My own techniques for success developed and stemmed from a very young age, whilst I was still at school. I enjoyed entering art and coloring competitions – whatever I entered for, I won. My entries were modified or adapted to such an extent that they were very different from everyone else's, which appealed to my sense of humor and gave me such a sense of pride. My son also used the same ideas and methods (with a little guidance from mom) when he was younger, allowing him to also reap the rewards of success. He became so proficient at modifying his entries that he won the coloring competitions in our local newspaper nearly every week for a year. Eventually the newspaper editor cancelled the junior weekly competition slot after my son's winning streak was commented on by one of the many photographers who had been sent to our home to obtain a photo of the winning child with his prize. Shame on them for ruining his fun!

Perfecting the formula

After a lapse of about ten years, when I didn't enter any competitions whatsoever, I was persuaded to take up this exciting hobby again by a work colleague (to whom I remain indebted). I challenged myself to develop a successful technique based purely on the art of manipulation – if I do anything at all, I always strive for perfection. I found it very difficult to contain my excitement when I unexpectedly hit upon the correct formula in local and national competitions; I found myself winning a high proportion of the prizes that I entered for. This winning streak has continued without a break.

Cheap days out

Today, as I write this for you, I have received another prize; a pair of tickets for a concert held at the magnificent Winchester Cathedral, one of my all-time favorite locations. This win was via a local newspaper (thank you!). The cost to me? A postage stamp and a recycled postcard – oh, how I love this hobby!

We were all beginners once

There is no real reason why the winner shouldn't be you, is there? Don't talk yourself out of entering any competition that appeals to you. Why should someone else win the prize that you can visualize yourself winning? You need to convince yourself that you can and will succeed at everything you do from this moment onward. As long as you have fulfilled the basic entry requirements (check the details carefully), you too stand a very good chance of winning the prize of your dreams. Remember – all the experts and regular winners were beginners once. We are not born with the skills that we need to win the best prizes; they need to be learned, practiced and adapted.

PRIZE T!P
Keep reminding yourself: "If I'm in, there's a chance I'll win."

Check out the prize list

There is usually more than one prize in a competition – carefully check the details of what is on offer. Prizes do not always reflect the promoter's own products, for example a toilet roll manufacturer could be offering a holiday or pampering session among the prizes, so I advise you not to disregard any competition leaflets without reading them thoroughly.

First and second prize winners

A second prize win is not always second-best in terms of value or usefulness to the recipient. Some of my favorite wins have been 'runner up' prizes; soon, with time and experience, you will be able to target the level of prize that you prefer to win.

Make the prize yours

An example of selecting a preferred prize is when my young son won the opportunity of a 'trolley dash' at Legoland (toy manufacturers) several years ago, courtesy of a local newspaper. All of the ten finalists were invited to take part in a tie-breaker at the Legoland site in Windsor, London; at that stage they were all 'regional winners', though their exact prize had not been determined. The nine 'runners up' each received a tour of the model makers' workshops instead of the trolley dash, which was exactly the prize that my son wanted. He deliberately lingered behind after the official tour, and made useful staff contacts during that time, leading to several further invites for exclusive 'money-can't-buy' experiences of follow-up visits to see the staff he originally met and befriended on the prize tour. It was his 'dream come true'; if he can achieve it, then you too can manipulate a prize in your favor.

Gaining confidence

Initially you might be lacking in confidence, not knowing quite how to get started. I imagine that in the past you might even have talked yourself out of entering the high value competitions in the mistaken belief that someone else is more qualified, and therefore more likely, in some way, to win the prize instead of you – this is a normal reaction, a way of protecting yourself from disappointment. Once you have learned the basic skills, and have had a few small wins, you will find that your confidence and enthusiasm will grow rapidly. Aim as high as you dare to.

Dwell on it

Success breeds success – if you are in a positive frame of mind, then your competition entries are likely to reflect this. Capture the feeling of elation that you get when you open a letter informing you that you're a winner, and imagine it happening again as you write your slogan or decorate your postcard. Remember: the prize could be yours already; you just need to entice the judge to select your entry once the deadline has passed. It might sound too easy, but you really can enhance your chances of winning.

Note the percentage rise

You will not win a prize every time you enter a competition, but you should be able to see the overall percentage of wins increasing as you gain knowledge, confidence and experience. Make a note of which competitions you have entered and what you have won – you might surprise yourself. It will take a while to establish a niche for your talents, but the journey will be an enjoyable one.

To share, or not to share?

Don't be surprised when your friends and work colleagues recognize the worth or value of keeping your acquaintance as news of your success spreads. The chances are that they will be keen to share in your success and help you cash in on your newly-developed skills. Several of them may even inundate you with entry forms for prizes they think you'll appreciate. There will undoubtedly be ulterior motives in this act of kindness; they may be harboring secret hopes of sharing any significant winnings with you. By all means, encourage and gratefully accept well-intentioned offers of help, but make sure that you don't make promises that can't be kept. Holidays and meals out at fancy restaurants might lend themselves to being shared with other people, but what about a refrigerator or a day at the local health club?

Are you an amateur or a professional?

There is a very subtle difference between being an amateur comper or a professional; one that needs careful consideration as you set out on your journey to become a successful prize-winner. The difference is the amount of monetary income you generate from your hobby.

If your normal employment is in advertising, photography, art or writing, you might have difficulty convincing your country's tax authorities that a cash prize earned from your hobby is not an extension of your day job. The trick is to avoid competitions with cash prizes that overlap with the skills you use in your paid profession, i.e. photographers and artists should avoid entering competitions that incorporate photographic or visual elements, likewise, self-employed writers and advertising professionals should avoid entering writing or slogan competitions. It is best to play safe and enjoy your hobby rather than setting yourself up for an unnecessary tax bill.

Having said that, there is absolutely no harm in producing an entry to a polished, professional-like standard, because after all, we all should be striving to submit our very best work to a competition; only the best will win.

There may be a time when you do wish to become a full-time comper. As long as you keep a list of your earnings and declare it on your annual Income Tax or Inland Revenue return, there will not be a problem. Different countries have different rules and regulations you must adhere to.

Tax concerns – tax payers from the USA and Canada

Prize winners from the USA and Canada are subject to slightly different tax laws from their UK counterparts. At the time of writing, tax payers from the USA are required to declare a 'fair' market value of any prizes that have been won as taxable income on annual tax returns. Other countries may have similar tax laws and arrangements. Your interpretation of the fair market value and what you actually declare on your tax return is your responsibility. If in doubt, ask the competition organizer for a letter with an estimate of the value of the prize you have been awarded, or keep ticket stubs for events you have attended.

Complimentary event tickets might show a zero price/value (i.e. $0.00, £0.00 or €0.00); I suggest you photocopy these for your records before you use them. Events and experiences that are not ticketed or not offered for sale to the public are a separate issue; you are unlikely to be able to assign an accurate value to these. If you are in any doubt about what you do and don't need to declare on your tax return, I suggest you contact your Inland Revenue Service office (IRS) and ask for advice. Canadian tax payers will need to contact the Canada Revenue Agency (CRA) for advice.

Inland Revenue Service (USA):

Website: http://www.irs.gov/

Help Desk: dial (800) 876-1715 toll-free from within the United States and Canada

Canadian Revenue Agency:

Website: http://www.cra-arc.gc.ca

Help Desk: dial 1-800-959-8281

Tax concerns – UK tax payers

Here's the really good news: in the United Kingdom (at the time of writing), prizes won by non-professional competitors in consumer competitions are generally considered to be tax-free for the winner. Premium bonds are tax-free. I have never heard of a UK comper having to pay any tax on prizes that have been won. Bear in mind though, that if a promoter requires you to do something substantial before or after you receive your prize, then the tax implications are likely to be different, since you are entering a business transaction. If in doubt, please contact your local HM Revenue & Customs office for further advice.

Contact details for the HM Revenue & Customs office dealing with your tax collection can be found on your annual P60 (for employed people) or on your annual tax coding letter. This is not always the office closest to where you live – it relates to the area the company you work for is registered.

For general advice see the National HM Revenue & Customs website: www.hmrc.gov.uk/index.htm

Cheap presents

If you win prizes with the intention of giving them away to friends and family, then it is probably in your interests not to tell your intended recipients where you acquired the presents from, especially if they're intended as Christmas or birthday gifts – you don't want to earn the reputation of being a cheapskate!

PRIZE T!P

In order to have the best chance of reaping rewards it is advisable to start by entering local competitions rather than the well-publicized national competitions. By 'starting local' you will be competing against far fewer entrants. Techniques for improving your success rate will be introduced in subsequent chapters of this book.

Essential equipment

Like any hobby, there are a few essential items that you will need to acquire. This kit will be relatively inexpensive; most items are things that you might already have at home. Almost certainly, your first small win should cover the cost of everything you need. Add to your kit as your enthusiasm and success grows. I suggest that you keep these together, perhaps in a special box, a drawer or a bureau so that they are readily available whenever you see a competition that you wish to enter.

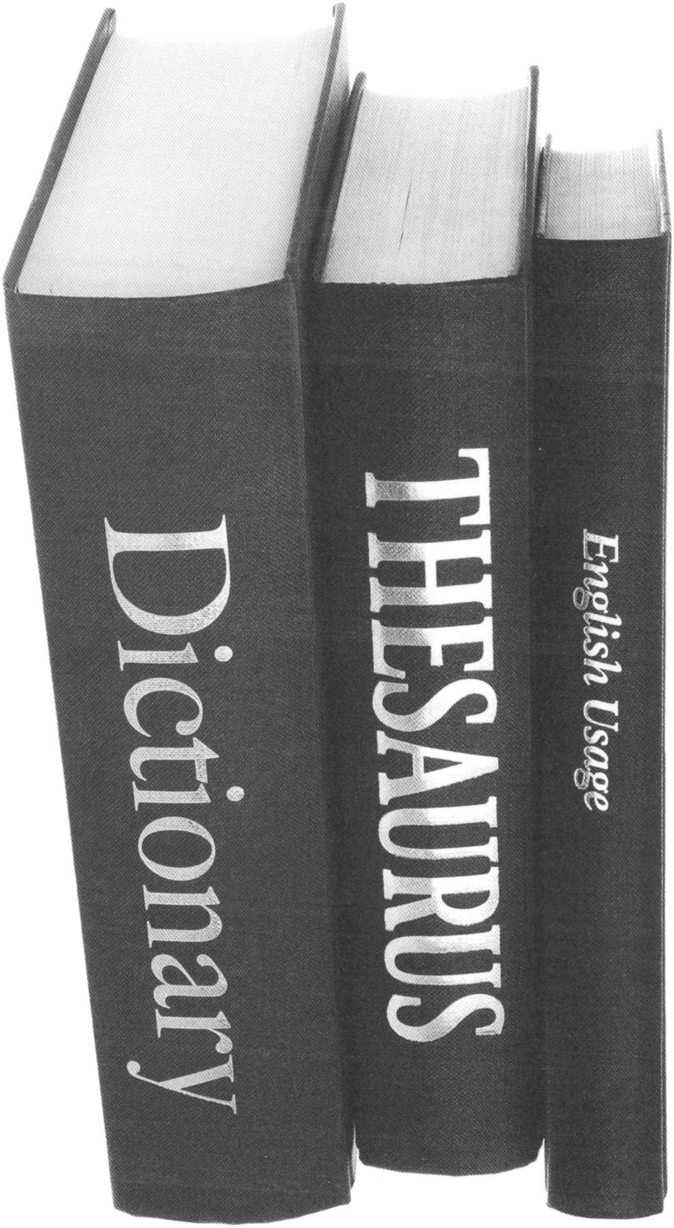
Dictionary
THESAURUS
English Usage

The competitor's toolkit

- A selection of brightly colored envelopes, various sizes

- Plain white envelopes, various sizes

- Pens (several colors)

- Highlighter pens

- Colored pencils or crayons

- Stickers or decorative inked stampers (you can obtain these from most stationers, art and craft stores or toy stores)

- Full-colored postcards, small and large

- A thesaurus (advisable)

- Scissors, straight cut as well as patterned-effect cut

- Sticky tape or a glue stick

- A stapler

- Postage stamps

- A small notebook (this is useful for recording your slogan ideas in)

Entry Forms and Details

" Anybody can win –
unless there happens to be
a second entry. **"**

George Ade

Chapter 2
Entry Forms and Details

Superb! You've made the decision that you want to become proficient at entering and winning competitions, and have assembled the correct equipment – all you need now is a competition to enter.

Choosing the format

There is a huge array of competition formats available to competitors at the moment, ranging from simple prize draws and puzzles to those that require extensive research and tie-breaker slogans. Ploughing your way through the multitude of options can be quite bewildering at first, though you'll soon grasp the basics. You may already have an inkling of which type of competition suits your personal style, and may even have dabbled at entering a few contests in the past. Armed with a selection of effective comping tools you should be able to change your success rate and gain much deserved personal satisfaction.

Prize value versus method

The lower value prizes are often prize draws, instant wins, crosswords and puzzles, whereas very high value prizes often require you to write a relevant, witty slogan or tie-breaker. If you are lucky, you might even see your slogan being incorporated in the promoter's future advertising campaigns.

Mode of entry

The mode of entry could be a postcard, an entry form, via a website address, or even by a lengthy call to a premium telephone number. You will often need to buy a product and produce the sales receipt as a 'qualifier' if the competition is sourced through a store or other commercial outlet. Newspapers and in-house newsletters and magazines usually require nothing more from you than an entry coupon (to prove that you have bought a copy) or your address details via a letter, an email or a postcard. There are no hard and fast rules to this – it is entirely at the promoter's discretion.

Radio star

An increasingly popular form of competition is the local radio station 'phone-in' which requires the listener to identify a voice, part of a song or the year in which a medley of songs played were originally released. You will need to be quick off the mark to stand a chance of success with this – most of the telephone lines available on the switchboard will be jammed within seconds of the 'lines open' announcement. There will probably be twenty or more callers queuing – usually only one will be randomly selected to answer the question on air. If the answer is incorrect, another will be chosen. Eventually a winner will be announced. The prizes are usually worth winning, sponsored by local businesses who use the radio media for advertising.

Adapt your talents

The choice is yours – you need to start somewhere, though I do suggest that you concentrate on utilizing and adapting any talents you already possess in the first instance (for example in solving crosswords or writing amusing ditties) then building up your skills-base gradually. You will probably find that the learning process is quite exciting. Armed with the best secrets in the trade, it won't be long before you find a niche for yourself in the local prize-winning stakes.

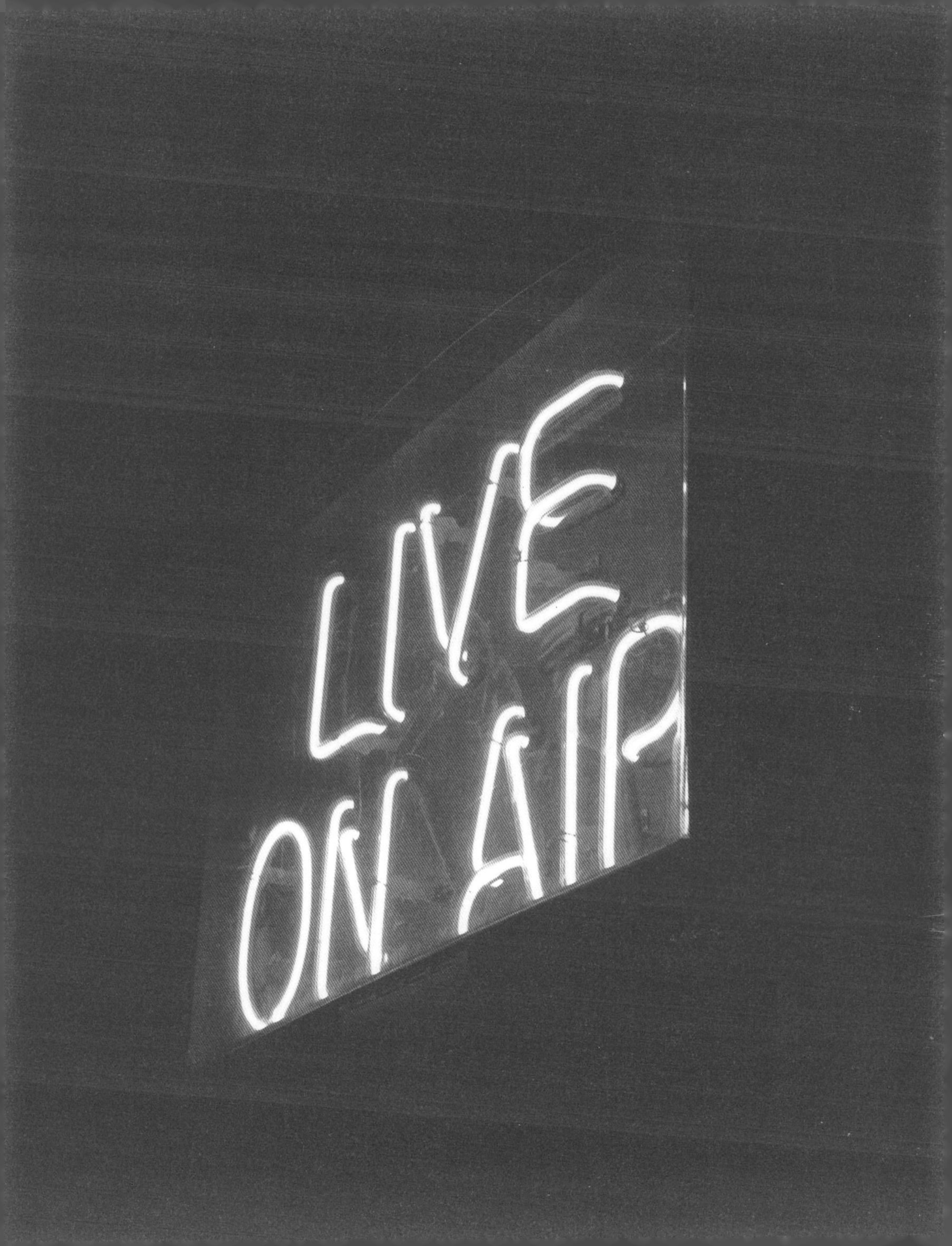
LIVE
ON AIR

Where to find leaflets with entry forms

First you need to decide upon which style of competition you wish to enter, as this will affect the location of the entry forms. Most hobby compers use a mixture of methods to secure their dream prizes and are opportunistic in their approach to looking for forms. You don't need to be a serious fanatic when searching for competition entry forms – the likelihood is that after a short while, you'll hone in on them with no obvious effort on your part.

Supermarkets are competition-leaflet heaven; you just need to know where to look for them. The regular way of displaying these is in transparent leaflet holders in front of the product that they are advertising, check also at the customer service desk. Sometimes you need a little perseverance in hunting down the more elusive entry forms in various stores, though you will soon develop a knack for spotting a competition leaflet from the end of a crowded shopping aisle.

Fuelling the addiction

You might be inclined to organize your shopping sprees so that you target certain stores that you know are holding competitions at the time – it is at this point that you can truly class yourself as a 'comping addict'.

Check before you buy

Check the closing date for entries in the small print of the rules section on the leaflet before you buy any product that you need to produce a sales receipt for; many shops fail to remove old, expired leaflets, so you could end up wasting your money unnecessarily.

Reduce the leaflet supply

If you have had difficulty locating your entry forms, then no doubt, other people will have experienced the same problems. One way of reducing the number of entries in a competition is to grab a handful of forms whenever you find them, even if the rules limit you to just one entry. After all, if other people cannot find an entry form, they cannot enter the competition; you will have increased your chance of winning before you have even entered. It really is being quite mean, isn't it? Don't worry – bear in mind that you will not be the only comper doing this; it is common practice. You might get a few disapproving looks if you take them all, but you'll soon become immune to them. If you feel too guilty to grab more than a couple of entry forms or leaflets at a time, ask other friends or family members to collect some for you, 'every little helps' (as one well-known supermarket slogan proudly states).

Do you need to buy a qualifier?

If the specified prizes tempt you, then you'll need to establish whether or not you need to attach a product receipt or label to your entry form; this is known as the 'qualifier'. Fortunately, many promotions state 'no purchase necessary' with the promoter just hoping that you'll buy the product if you enter the competition, however, most are not that trusting. If you do need to buy the product, then segregate it from the rest of your shopping at the cash desk and get a separate receipt for each item. You might possibly need to retain your other main sales receipt for unrelated product guarantee purposes, which is a problem if you have sent it off with your competition entry (as competition qualifiers are not returned to you). Don't worry about the annoyance you cause to other waiting customers at the cash desk; many people segregate food items for other reasons – you shouldn't feel at all guilty about it.

Delay your purchase

You may have seen details of a competition that you wish to enter advertised in the national media or in various competition club magazines. You might even have prepared a slogan in readiness for submitting your entry, but one thing that you can be almost certain of is that you cannot enter without obtaining the appropriate entry form. If you need to attach the sales receipt for a qualifier item, then it is advisable to delay your purchase until the entry form is in your possession. Unfortunately, not all branches of national stores will choose to stock the entry forms or leaflets that you are searching for.

Various forms of qualifiers

Not all qualifiers are in the form of receipts or labels – use your ingenuity if the qualifier is for an item that you either cannot find on the shelf, or are unlikely to ever use. In these circumstances you might know somebody who can provide the suitable qualifier for you (for example if you are a vegetarian and would be required to purchase meat-based products). I won a holiday courtesy of the 'Diet Coke' drinks manufacturer a few years ago: my friend gave me the leaflet with the entry form on, all I required was a ring-pull from a can of Diet Coke (which I picked up from the floor in a car park), and to write a witty slogan about why I liked the product.

Time for posting

Now that you have obtained your entry form and qualifier, you should be ready to enter the competition. If it is a draw-style contest, use a brightly colored envelope if possible, (especially if you have to include two or more qualifier proof items) or a large postcard (not suitable if you need to attach a long receipt). For slogans, plain white envelopes are all that are required, as each entry will be individually opened and read by a member of the judging team.

Keeping your sales receipts

Keep all of your sales receipts – you never know when they will be useful. Perhaps you could ask your friends for theirs as well if there is a high-value competition that you wish to submit several entries for, or if you know that they buy unusual items in stores that you rarely shop at. Each entry form will usually require a separate receipt or a qualifier item to be attached to it.

Receipts with timed-purchase restrictions

Competition qualifier products that you can highlight or circle on a receipt do not always need to be recently bought items (I regularly use receipts that are up to a year old), but almost certainly will need to be for a particular size of the specified item i.e. a 14oz (400g) can of soup, or a six-bottle pack of beer. Using previously bought receipted items could save you a lot of extra expense and effort, and really does work – the organizers are seldom bothered as to when you made your purchase, just as long as you have done so. Occasionally there will be a timed-purchase stipulation in the competition entry details, so you will need to check this carefully.

PRIZE T!P
In the interest of avoiding fraudulent use of your financial and personal information, always delete credit or debit card details from the receipts with thick black marker pen, or pay for your items using cash. Once you send the sales receipts to the competition organizer (or competition 'clearinghouse') it is too late – they will not be returned to you.

Information leaflets

Not all competition leaflets will contain an entry coupon or a form for you to fill out. These often offer you the opportunity to send your details by postcard, letter, phone text message, premium rate phone call, plain-paper entry, or via a website. Read the details carefully, as the postal address may differ from the promoter's address.

Website referrals

Leaflets might refer you to a website address in order to download an entry form, or complete your details online. It is advisable to check the terms and conditions that will appear as a hyperlink (in most cases). Unless you intentionally opt out of receiving the promoter's marketing information (look for tick boxes in the small print), you will probably receive regular email newsletters if you enter competitions by this method.

Leaflet small print

There will often be boxes for you to complete with your daytime phone contact details and email address on entry forms. Check the small print in the terms and conditions to determine how and when you will be contacted if you are a prize winner. If notification is by post, and it doesn't state that these extra details are essential to enter the competition, then make your choice as to whether you wish to provide them. I often write 'ex-directory' in the phone column, and 'none' in the email section; prizes have still been awarded to me, without my having received unwanted marketing material by phone or email. The choice is yours.

Local newspaper competitions

The easiest way for you to get started on your quest for prizes is to seek out all the minor prize draws from your local newspaper; the chances are that you probably already buy it every week and have overlooked the many opportunities available to you. These are likely to have very short entry deadlines – possibly as short as a week to meet their circulation or printing schedules, so you will need to have a selection of full-color postcards, envelopes and postage stamps available in readiness to enter quickly.

Local versus national newspapers

Local newspaper competitions tend to be promoted by local suppliers, and are of the prize-draw type; at most, there might be a few hundred entries, which is considerably less than you will expect for the national tabloids. Post two entries for each competition if the rules permit; post them on separate days to ensure that they arrive on different days, and will therefore be in different positions in the competition bag. Post one of them on the day that the newspaper goes on sale if possible, so that you do not miss any deadline (which is often not stated).

PRIZE T!P

Make sure the prize is something you actually want, and can make use of, for example, if the prize is flight tickets check that you are available to use them before you enter. Holidays and flights are often not transferable to another person or may be date specific.

Collecting your prize

Many local newspapers assume that you live in the distribution area, and may occasionally expect you to collect your prize if it is heavy or bulky. Smaller items such as books, meal vouchers, CDs and event tickets will almost certainly be posted to you.

Junk mail

Before you dispose of the wads of leafleted junk mail you receive, sift through it all. Local businesses will sometimes entice new customers to try their products or services by offering prize draws. I have obtained meals out and numerous boxes of toiletries via this route. You will probably be asked to complete a coupon which you post 'in store' rather than sending by regular mail, as part of their ongoing advertising campaign. This might seem a little intimidating and off-putting, however, the number of entries they receive is likely to be very low, so you stand an excellent chance of winning. Just hand your form to the cashier if you cannot see a prominently-displayed competition box.

Entries needed please

One newspaper editor recently told me that she has floods of entries for the minor prizes, but very few for the larger, more-valuable prizes. She assumed that people thought they had less chance of winning the more prestigious items (which she declared to be the opposite of the real situation) and perhaps this is the reason they didn't submit their entries. She found this both surprising and quite disappointing.

Later sections of this book explain how you can improve the odds of winning these local competitions quite considerably. I win something nearly every week from my local newspapers, for very little effort, and a minimal number of entries. You could do this too.

Take slogans with you

Always carry a slogan crib sheet when you go shopping or to publicized events; you never know when or where it will be useful. Your crib sheet could include a selection of 'winning' favorite slogans that can be rapidly adapted. This confers a huge advantage to you, as your entry will stand out from all of the other childish 'on-the-spot' sentences or quips that most people will produce when they're in a hurry. The entry deadline will usually be limited to the day of the event.

Use your notebook

Every good comper should have a notebook and pencil to hand. When out shopping or socializing you might see posters with web-based competition addresses or overhear clever phrases which you could use elsewhere. You might even get an insider viewpoint on what the promoter is looking for whilst casually talking to a store assistant when paying for your purchases. Be bold, flirty, or whatever it takes, as long as you manage to ask a few relevant questions (without letting on that you're actually interested in entering) – believe me, it really does work wonders; I do it all the time.

Don't rely on your memory – jot everything down in your notebook as soon as you get out of the store so that you can get your competition entries filled out as soon as you return home. If it is a 'post-in-store' competition, I suggest you ask a friend to deliver it for you, so that you are not immediately recognized by the same store assistant.

Adapt and win

If there has been some advance publicity for the store-opening event, then you might also have to hand in a coupon that has been printed in the local newspaper – try taping it to the back of a postcard or a photo. Take scissors, postcards and sticky tape with you if the day has been advertised on radio rather than in newspapers or by leaflet drops in your home area. Other techniques you can use to good effect are using a fluorescent envelope for your coupon, or folding it into a concertina pattern – these alter the appearance or texture of your competition entry, especially as someone will probably mix them all by hand before lifting one out of the box. I once won a 4ft high Coca Cola brand soft-toy polar bear for my son (who was four years old at the time) by this method. I'm sure you can imagine the squeals of delight when I arrived home with a bear that was taller than him!

Instant wins

Instant win prizes can be found inside wrappers (food and sweets are common), and under bottle caps. These might show a code number which will usually refer to a list which is printed on the outside of the product wrapper or container, or can be checked on the promoter's website or could require you to phone a 'hotline number' to reveal whether or not you are a winner. I always avoid the latter, as you could spend more on the phone call than either the prize or the original product is worth.

Are there any prizes left?

The products displaying 'instant win' competitions will almost certainly have pre-printed, pre-determined winning packages, and cannot be manipulated in your favor. It is highly likely that all prizes will have been claimed before consumers have purchased all of the stock remaining on the store shelves throughout the country.

Cookie torment

Another option for checking the code and claiming your prize is via a website; this could lead to unwanted 'cookies' being installed on your system, or unwanted advertising spam targeting your private email address. If you are happy to use an email address for this purpose, I suggest using a temporary/disposable email address such as a 'hotmail' or similar, which you can check via an online web server. It is best to avoid using your normal personal or work email addresses owing to the likelihood of spam messages being received.

PRIZE T!P

Look out for competitions advertised in store windows. These might be advertised by a poster or by a prominent window display. It is likely that this type of competition will have a very short deadline. Have your slogan list prepared and handy when you go shopping, as this will give you an advantage over other shoppers if a slogan is required.

Check your diary

If the rules state that the prize will be on a specific date and time, make sure you can be there, or any prize that you may have been in contention for could be forfeit and awarded to somebody else. I have seen this happen too many times.

Photography

Details of specialist competitions such as photography, garden design and those with literary themes will be found in the relevant magazines or leaflets in specialist sales outlets.

Photographic retailers usually have an in-store magazine, and will often promote their contests through this media. Photographic image submission to a competition will require you to declare that you are the copyright owner.

Gardening

Garden centers and DIY stores will either use their quarterly magazines to advertise their large garden design competitions, or you might find the details printed directly on the sponsor's own garden maintenance product labels. These are quite rare.

Seed suppliers tend to offer annual slogan competitions – look amongst the seed packets at the beginning of spring when the new 'planting season' starts.

Recipe competitions

Magazines and a few culinary suppliers (look on jar labels) will feature this type of competition, usually to celebrate a specific occasion, such as Mother's Day. This is ideal for adults and children (who should be supervised when cooking).

Tried and tested

We've all got cookery books that gather dust in a bookcase; these are valuable resources when it comes to designing and perfecting your own recipes. Look for a recipe that grabs your attention in some way. It should be relatively simple to prepare, should be good value for money, and above all, must be colorful. A slight tweak to an ingredient list might be all that you need. To win, your meal must appeal to a wide audience, and look stunning (without appearing to be complicated or overly fussy).

Photograph your meal

When you have perfected your meal, take a photograph, as some competitions require this (especially magazines); this must look artistic, so select your serving plate and background carefully. Hopefully, you will be invited to share your expertise at a cook-off; this could be immense fun, even if you do not win the overall first prize. Savor the experience.

Children's magazines

Magazines targeted at parents of pre-school and primary-school age children are rife with competitions to win toys, especially around Christmas time. Enter these in your own name, and then you can choose whether to offer the prize to your child as a birthday or Christmas present, or simply to give it as a surprise gift or a reward (at a time of your choosing).

Children's coloring competitions

Coloring competitions will often require parental assistance for very young children, especially if handling paints or fibre-tipped pens. Most organizers accept that assistance is required for safety reasons (such as eating pens or drawing on the walls), however, the work should predominantly be that of your child. There is no pleasure in cheating (we've all met pushy parents, haven't we?) though we all get involved in helping to a certain extent.

Add artistic detail

If you help your child to alter the outlines of the template and add a little more detail to the picture itself for your child before he or she colors it in, there's a much-enhanced possibility that your child is in with a good chance of winning. The judge is bound to be impressed with the extra effort that makes the picture different from the pile of identical badly-colored entries, especially if it obvious that the child has made the amendments him or herself. I must confess to suggesting further improvements for my son's entries on a few occasions, after he thought he had finished them.

Alter the texture

Try using glitter and other 'collage' materials for extra textural effect. Avoid using felt-tip pens, as they can easily soak through the paper and give a very messy end result; a much better effect is obtained by using colored pencil crayons or watercolor crayons (which are applied dry and blended with a small amount of water at the end stage).

A camera and vitamin pills!

The strangest prize package that my son won via a coloring competition (when he was eleven years old) was a digital camera accompanied by three packs of orange-flavored vitamin pills. Surprisingly, he loved the vitamin pills and has demanded that I buy them for him ever since... the advertiser's promotion via the competition obviously worked!

Children's freestyle paintings

Your child may wish to enter painting (as opposed to coloring) competitions. You might have just one entry form, so do you take the risk of letting your junior Picasso ruin his or her chances of winning one of the prizes? No, I thought not! When I used to support my own child in his desire to enter this style of competition, we used to practice painting the required design onto large hand-drawn copies or photocopies of the entry form prior to producing the finished article. We would then choose the best one to re-do and enter into the competition. It certainly saved many tears of frustration.

No children? Don't enter

If you don't have a child, I suggest you don't enter competitions in your own name that are intended for children (knowing how much ladies like to lie about their age), as you may well have to collect your prize in person. If all else fails... enter on behalf of a friend's child. Obviously, you should seek permission before you do this. Be nice – let the child keep the prize!

Only one entry allowed per person

If you have two or more first names, and there is only one entry per person, then try entering in all of your names. Do this for each member of your family if you are really desperate to win a particular prize. You might be able to get away with this if you do not have to list dates of birth. You may be restricted to a 'one prize per household' rule, which is a common clause.

PRIZE T!P

For 'one entry per household' competitions, if a child lives with only one of his/her parents you should be able to enter from both parents' addresses if they give permission. You might even strike lucky and win twice (one from each address).

Women's magazines

Popular women's magazines often feature many phone-in competitions for holidays, and luxury 'must have' fashion accessories and items. Check the phone tariff details and the possible duration of the call before you enter. Contests are likely to be 'simple' in nature, and often rely on a large volume of correct-answer calls, which cover the cost of the prize, (similar to those advertised on television after specific programmes). It is easy to be duped by this. Not all magazines fall into this category, but do be aware that the odds of winning are very low. Do not use your cell phone, as the rates are higher than for a landline. Ideally, enter by a postal method if the option is available.

School newsletters

School newsletters might feature seasonal contests for the pupils – entries are usually subject to much apathy, so your child will have a very good chance of winning. Your child will usually need to collect a specific entry form from a member of staff before they can enter the competition –

advise them to do this. If they are too shy, send a note to school with your child, requesting that a form is sent home. My past employment as a secondary school teacher gave me an excellent insight to the reasons why children don't enter; most of it is peer pressure or ridicule amongst school friends.

School competitions

Designing posters, logos, word searches, quizzes and Christmas cards are all regular topics, as well as coloring competitions, attracting as few as a dozen entries in most cases, usually from the younger children. There might be a nominal small entry fee to cover any administration costs (such a photocopying), or a contribution to school funds. Entering any of these competitions will almost certainly secure a prize or a reward certificate. There is nothing to prevent you from 'helping' your child to complete the task, but try not to make it too obvious, as your school staff will already have an appreciation of the child's standard of work.

Workplace magazines

Workplace magazines are another source of unusual styles of competition – the 'add a caption' to an embarrassing photo type of tie-breaker. The winning captions are usually amusing and fictitious rather than factual. Be careful with these, especially if the photo is of another company employee; it is incredibly easy to cause long-lasting offence with work colleagues. Prize crosswords, Sudoku, quizzes and puzzles are regular features of this type of newsletter, and well worth entering (if only for the prestige of out-smarting the boss!).

Form swapping

Why not exchange entry forms with your other comping enthusiast friends? This is especially useful if you live in different towns. If there is specific local information that your friend has access to that you require before you can enter the competition, ask for it. This is a two-way process, and can be mutually beneficial, so try to use it. I have lost count of the number of 'extra' prizes that I have gained by this method.

File it

A useful item to include in your equipment list is a concertina file which has twelve compartments. Label each compartment with a different month of the year, and store your entry forms there until a few weeks before the competition deadline date. The work that you have spent time and effort preparing is likely to sit at the bottom of the competition collection box if you post it off too early, so try to submit your entries no earlier than about 14 days before the final closing date – that way they'll be higher in the judging pile, and possibly more likely to catch the judge's attention.

Everything must go

Officially, all of the advertised prizes have to be awarded unless the situation occurs where there are more prizes available than the number of entries that are submitted.

Ex-directory telephone numbers

If you do not wish to receive advertising material from the competition promoters, or you have a telephone number that is ex-directory, I advise you to mark this clearly on your entry form, write it on your postcard submission, or tick any 'no marketing' small-print boxes if they are available. Use your common sense with this though, and consider whether or not you wish to offer your phone details at all (this information is necessary in some cases for notifying you of your win – read the competition rules carefully).

Improving the odds in your favor

After you have checked the entry rules, and have established that either an envelope or plain paper entry is not an absolute requirement, you can set about increasing your odds of success.

The odds of winning will vary with the type of competition you are entering. Fewer people will enter slogan competitions than prize draws, and even less will enter competitions that require you to make a purchase of an expensive item. You have an improved chance of success with local contests versus national ones; suggestions on how best to tackle these will be given later.

What's in it for the promoters?

It appears that the commercial world is gripped by competition fever – it's such an easy way to promote consumer products, with very low advertising costs, to a receptive, enthusiastic audience. How better to capture the average shopper's imagination and willingness to buy a product that wouldn't normally be on the weekly shopping list than with the lure of winning a luxury prize? Everyone loves to receive luxury items free of charge. The resulting high profile newspaper or magazine publicity of the competition sponsors handing a prize to an excited winner is an excellent excuse for a public relations exercise, and is usually snapped up free of charge by eager journalists. It is a win-win situation for everyone involved.

Publicity events

There is often a clause in the competition entry details that specifies that entrants must be willing to take part in publicity photos or events. Check the details carefully, and make sure you are available for any dates that are specified. More often than not, you will not be forced to attend, but if you are formally requested to do so, I advise you to go along to collect your prize. The whole publicity experience is usually great fun – you will certainly be well-pampered, and could even come away with more goodies than you expected. There could also be more instant draws on the day for any unclaimed prizes.

Summary – locating competition details

- Leaflets in supermarkets and stores

- Stores' own magazines

- Local and national newspapers

- School newsletters

- Workplace newsletters

- Websites

- Store-opening events

- Junk mail delivered to your home

- Women's magazines

- Children's magazines and comics

- Specialist retail outlets

- Swapping with other competition enthusiasts

Customizing
Your Entry

“ Competitions are what you do as a good exercise. **”**

Maya Lin

Chapter 3
Customizing Your Entry

You've seen the prize you want to win, but there's a problem – too many other entrants! What you need now is a way to customize your entry and increase your chances of winning. Absorb the tips recommended to you in this chapter, prepare your entries and get them posted. There's no need to cross your fingers; contrary to popular belief, it doesn't bring you good luck, it just brings pain...

The art of manipulation

There is a lot of underlying psychology related to the 'art' of winning the lucky dip style of prize draws. Big gains can be made by using a cunning array of simple, effective mental-manipulation techniques to make your entry appear to be more visually prominent, be it a postcard or an envelope, and therefore ultimately making it more selectable. If you have the time and enthusiasm, I suggest that you customize your entry; why waste a postage stamp on something that is unlikely to win anything?

And the winner is...

If your entry is picked out, you have to be awarded the prize, that's the governing rule and must be adhered by; even if the judge recognizes your name and address (they must be fairly fed up with me by now). Officially, once a winner has been drawn and identified in this manner, the entry cannot be placed back in the box for an alternative winner to be drawn out. This is probably one of the reasons why new competitors assume that competitions are 'rigged', simply because the same winners' names keep appearing in the published results lists.

Be cunning, be colorful

If you consider the judge's task, he or she will undoubtedly be required to select at least one winner from a possible bag or box full of entries, which may be in a multitude of formats; envelopes of various colors, plain and not-so-plain postcards. Which of these do you think is likely to attract a judge's attention the quickest?

The majority of ordinary people who will have spotted the competition, and fancy their chances of winning, will be unlikely to possess anything other than standard DL or C6 sized white envelopes or the standard small white postcards that can be bought in the newsagent or the Post Office. These drab, plain postcards and envelopes will form the bulk of the large sack of entries. Your entry needs to stand out from the rest – this is even more important if only one prize is up for grabs. Consider the prize to be yours already – all you need to do is to persuade the judge to choose your entry. Manipulating the odds in your favor is easier than you might think.

Grab a postcard

You can obtain good quality full-color postcards from a variety of sources reasonably inexpensively; shops in tourist locations, Post Offices, newsagents, cinemas and hotel receptions are a few examples. Of this list I prefer the cinema option, especially as they are often displayed for advertising or promotional purposes, and can usually be obtained free of charge (check next time you go, or make a special visit and grab a large handful to make your journey worthwhile!). Ignore the neutral-colored, uninteresting postcards – the brightest and silliest ones are always the prime winning material.

A sense of humor

If a picture on a postcard makes you chuckle out loud to yourself, then it will probably have the same effect on somebody else. The image can be saucy, but please make sure it's not blatantly rude, as this will be deemed to be inappropriate, and could cause offence. One of my favorite images is that of a man sitting in a bath, wearing a bikini, and being hose-piped with orange juice. Thankfully, it appears that the judges must have liked it too...

Color matters

A highly colored card amongst all of the white envelopes and white postcards will be instantly obvious to the judge if it is 'face up', and is not buried too deep underneath others. If your card is upside down, then it will look like all of the others (addresses and a stamp), conferring you no advantage. If you have plenty of time to be creative you can remedy this issue.

Be creative

Just think, if you are able to capture the judge's attention with either side of your postcard, then your chance of success will instantly be doubled when compared with other entrants – this is where your artistic talents will come in useful. Highlighter pens and high-visibility stickers will become part of your essential toolkit.

PRIZE T!P
KEEP IT LEGIBLE
The first rule is to write legibly. All illegible entries will automatically be disqualified; if your handwriting is indecipherable then it is impossible for your prize to be sent to you.

Angle your details

I always write my own address details at 45° or even 90° to the postal address I am sending my entry to, mainly because during the early stages of entering this type of competition I had quite a few entries returned to me accidentally by the Post Office sorting system. I imagine that since all writing is now on one side of the postcard, (unless you use the really cheap double white-sided cards) that confusion can arise with automated zip code recognition systems. Don't rely on your envelopes and postcards being hand-sorted at the mail sorting office – each of your competition entries must be capable of reaching the destination if they are to be prize-winners.

Splash on some highlighter

Try surrounding your answer and contact details with a highlighter pen, and notice how much of a difference it makes from close-up and also from a distance. I think you'll agree that it is really effective. Bright green, yellow or pink highlighter works best for this purpose.

Can you draw?

If you have time, then why not personalize the back of your postcard with a picture of the prize you hope to win (or cut out a photo of one and glue it on). Make it bright and prominent; the brighter it is, the more chance it has of being detected amongst all of the other plain entries in the sack.

Use stickers for decoration

I tend to alternate between drawing appropriate pictures next to my contact details and adding a sticker or two; frogs, birds, butterflies… whatever you wish. These are usually available in toy stores, discount stores and newsagents on strips of card, and are well worth investing in. Supermarkets, stationers and craft stores will also sell these, however, they will be more expensive than from other outlets – shop around for them. I generally cost them out at two or three stickers for the same cost as a postage stamp (or less of course).

Fragrant offerings

A few people will advise you to spray your entry with perfume – forget it! Think of the judge – is he or she really going to waste time sniffing the bag, and select the one postcard or envelope with the strongest smell? It just doesn't improve your chances of winning in prize draws, though it might possibly tip the decision with slogan tie-breakers when each entry is opened and read before a decision is made.

Recycling your Christmas cards as postcards

By far my best choice of postcard is the front of a Christmas card. Imagine being wished 'Happy Christmas', when it is still the middle of June… I have had a lot of wins by this method and cannot recommend more highly that you try it too. The more friends you've got, the more cards you'll receive, so send small cheap cards to people you don't really get on with at work, and get much nicer, bigger ones back (how mercenary of me!). Failing that – ask everyone for all of their cards when they've taken them down after Christmas, cut off the fronts, and recycle the backs. That is exactly what I do every year. If you can get your hands on them, the large corporate cards are the best for visual impact; there's plenty of space on the back for your artwork too.

Sparkle with tinsel

We all love tinsel at Christmas, don't we? But have you ever thought about using it in the middle of summer? January is a good time to head to the stores and buy up surplus Christmas decorations. The very thin tinsel and sparkly gift-wrapping ribbons are likely to be available at bargain prices and are ideal for decorating the edges of your prize-winning postcards and envelopes. Attach the tinsel or ribbon with craft glue or sticky tape for a really impressive effect.

Photos make great postcards

Interesting photos you have taken can also be used as postcards. Obtain large prints (on heavy card preferably); these are often just as good as the shop-bought item, and considerably cheaper as well. If your photos feature a person in an awkward or embarrassing predicament, then ideally you should ask their permission before you send their image to other people.

Attach your coupon

Entry forms that require you to complete a coupon can also be sent by this method – simply tape it to a postcard. Very few people will consider doing this; they will enclose it in an envelope instead, thus conferring an obvious advantage to you at the prize draw stage. If you send a picture postcard, it will be prominent amongst a pile of plain envelopes (irrespective of their color).

Multiple entries

As already mentioned in Chapter 1, I suggest submitting at least two entries if the rules allow you to do so. If it is the sort of competition that is likely to have a large number of submissions, then post them on different days, as these will naturally appear at different depths in the judge's bag, and will increase the chance of one being spotted easily.

Embarrassing moments

A word of warning – your highly customized entry may come back to haunt you… I recently had to collect a prize (a barbecue set with all accessories) from my local newspaper office, and had to sign that I had received my prize. To my acute embarrassment, my childlike drawing and over-use of pink highlighter pen on a cut-down (recycled) birthday card that I had submitted was displayed to everyone in the queue of people at the reception desk. A rude postcard would have been even worse! Never mind though, I had gained a much-wanted prize for the total cost of just one postage stamp.

" He who fears being conquered is sure of defeat. **"**

Napoleon Boneparte

A summary of tips for using postcards

- Always use full-colored postcards or the fronts of greeting/Christmas cards instead of plain white postcards

- Take care to write your entry details legibly or your entry will be disqualified

- Write your address details and any answers to questions at right angles to the entry address

- Use a highlighter or draw pictures to enhance the back of your postcard

- Use stickers on the back of your card if you have them

- Always use a postcard instead of an envelope if the rules allow you to do so

- If you have any amusing photos, get them printed onto card and use them

- Enter more than once if permitted – this increases your odds of being chosen

- Post your entry in good time, as delays do sometimes occur

- If you need to send a coupon, consider taping it to a postcard instead of using an envelope. Most people do not seem to use this method

National clearinghouse addresses

There are a few occasions where anything other than a plain white envelope is a waste of time, effort and money. These include: clearinghouse addresses (look out for 'NCH' (National Clearinghouse), Diss (Norfolk) or 'Nelson' when sending entries to a UK postal address) whenever you have to include a receipt or other qualifier item, e.g. a product label, and slogan entries. Clearinghouses will initially open all of the envelopes and place the correct and incorrect entries into separate piles before starting the process to select a winner. For all non-slogan or entries which are not being sent to clearinghouses, be as imaginative and creative with your envelope designs as possible!

Visualize yourself as a competition judge

By using a little psychology, you can increase your chances of winning quite dramatically. A good idea is to imagine yourself as a member of the judging panel, and then to visualize which factors would be most likely to influence you to select a particular envelope – you'll then be part way to success. You can even try this at home by placing all of your envelopes and postcards into a pile on the floor – which ones grab your attention the quickest? Use these to submit your entries with next time. Variations between all competitors' entries will be: color, size, decoration, handwriting style and postage stamps.

PRIZE T!P

If you need to use an envelope rather than a boldly-colored postcard for your entry form, then your choice of color and decoration can be a win or lose decision.

Colored envelopes

The most obvious advantage you have with envelope selection is the effect of color. Imagine that you are looking into a very large sack or box; all of the white and cream-colored envelopes, irrespective of size, will appear to merge together. A colored envelope will stand out from the rest; however, several competitors may have the same idea, especially after reading this book, in which case, there will be a smattering of color evident throughout the bag. Your envelope needs to be different from all of the other colored entries if it is to be picked out amongst the first three (for major prizes). So how can you maximize the effect? It is relatively easy with postcards, because your front image will be unique (hopefully), but how can you catch the judge's attention with an envelope? Simple, you must aim for yours to be bigger and brighter than everything else in the bag!

Fluorescent versus pastel shades

Trawl the shops for the brightest packs of envelopes that you can find, preferably in the larger sizes (choose the maximum size that can be sent with the cheapest value of postage stamps). Personally, I prefer to use the really bright fluorescent varieties rather than plain primary colors. I never opt for pastel shades (these merge to the same effect as white envelopes). It is obviously more cost-effective to purchase large rather than small packs, but these can be hard to find.

Black and sinister

I occasionally use black envelopes, with the address written in white correction fluid. I'm sure you'll agree that these have a very sinister look to them, yet they produce a definite 'wow' effect. The downside to writing in correction fluid is that it is extremely time-consuming. Black envelopes are rare to find and purchase, so do look out for them. If you see them, I suggest that you buy them straight away. Use these for Halloween-themed prizes. In contrast, bright red envelopes are excellent for Valentine's Day competitions.

Children's stationery packs

Another interesting slant on the use of colored envelopes is to purchase packs of kids' stationery, thereby saving yourself the effort of hand-decorating each entry. These packs usually contain pictured envelopes and writing paper, as well as a few pretty stickers that you can use elsewhere. Which judge wouldn't be swayed by what they think is a child's entry in preference to one from an adult? I know which I'd choose…

Decorate both sides of your envelope

If you opt for personalizing your envelopes, then remember that there are two sides available for your artwork if you have the time available. Consider using highlighter pens, inked stampers or stickers on either or both sides if you are short of time. I'm sure the postal sorting office staff won't thank you for it, but they are still obliged to deliver your letters.

Use distinctive lettering

When you write out the address, make it legible and neat, but with distinctive lettering. If you can make it look like a child's labored effort at writing, then the envelope might be selected out of sympathy! Remember, your design and lettering has to stand out from the rest of the competitors' entries, even if your envelope lands face upwards in the pile.

Postage stamp design

You can also make a difference with the type of postage stamp that you use – the pretty commemorative ones really can be quite attention-grabbing. I suggest that you buy these in bulk quantities as and when they are issued. They will probably only be available in loose-sheet form rather than the convenient self-adhesive book type, but it's well worth the inconvenience of licking the postage stamp. Large picture postage stamps are more distinctive than the smaller versions. Why not send Christmas stamps throughout the year? I regularly do this. Think – if someone spots your entry because it is out of season, and you cause them to smile, then you might possibly be in line for a prize already.

Make use of your printer

If you have a printer attached to your computer then you can use it to your advantage. Select a good photo, drawing or even an item of clip-art and use this to print your own envelope decorations. This method is much quicker and easier than manually decorating your envelopes. Remember to leave a white or clear space for the address details, and not to use any lettering that might interfere with the postal sorting machines when they try to read the zip code – after all, you do need it to be correctly delivered to the intended recipient.

Include a postcard

As long as the rules do not state that you have to send plain paper in an envelope, then you can place a postcard inside, which has your details written on it. This could capture the attention of a judge if all of the envelopes are opened in advance of the draw. This is likely to happen if address details are typed onto a marketing database. It is worth a try.

A summary of tips for using envelopes

- Use white envelopes for slogans or entries sent to clearinghouse addresses. All of these envelopes will be opened and checked before the winner phase of the competition takes place. For all other entries use colored envelopes if possible

- Buy kids' stationery packs to obtain ready-decorated envelopes. This saves you a lot of effort, especially if you are short of time

- Use large-sized colored envelopes (in preference to white or pastel shades) if they are available

- Decorate the front and backs of your entries with highlighter pens, stickers or inked stampers for the best effects

- If you have access to a computer printer, then you can use this to print personalized envelopes with photos, drawings or clip-art images

- Use the large pretty commemorative stamps in preference to standard postage stamps (especially those issued at Christmas)

Plain paper entries

There are a few instances where the entry rules stipulate that you must use a plain paper entry only, so just how plain does it need to be? I consider yellow, blue, fluorescent green and many other single-color papers to be of a plain color, and have won many prizes with this method. There are a few ways of attempting to beat the system, however you do need to ensure that you avoid disqualification by not trying to be 'too clever'. Many clearinghouses opt for the plain paper method. They will open all of the envelopes, check that any essential qualifiers have been included, and that the answers to any tie-breaker questions are correct before piling entries into the accept or reject piles.

Sending multiple plain paper entries

Some plain paper entry competitions will allow you more than one chance to enter, in which case, use one of every variation of color and technique to tempt the judges to select you as the winner. There are no guarantees that you will be successful, but being creative is certainly worth a try, though I suggest that your 'creativity' commences with your second or subsequent entries only.

The interesting rule bending that might occur is with prize draw competitions. Unless the rules clearly state plain 'white' paper, you might interpret plain as meaning anything except paper that has any form of pattern printed onto it, or cut into the edges with patterned-effect scissors. Do not use lined paper.

Change your handwriting style

Use an extra-wide-nibbed pen to write down your name and address details, and it will stand out much more than other entries that have used blue or black ballpoint pen on a white paper. The big marker pens are superb for this. Be really bold, and make your lettering really large and child-like for the maximum effect. If you are right-handed, then perhaps you could experiment with using your left hand for writing (and vice versa). My personal preference is using a pink or green highlighter pen on a contrasting color of paper. Try a few different techniques and see which of them catches your attention the quickest.

The size of paper

There is usually no limit to the size of paper that you are allowed to use – do check this in the rules. A small piece of paper is easily lost amongst a large pile of entries, so make sure your details are written clearly onto paper that is as big as you can practicably squeeze into an envelope. Forget your normal neatness and spatial awareness – make your writing extend right to each edge of the sheet so that your entry is always visible, even if it is partially tucked beneath others in the pile.

Slogans

If the competition requires you to submit a slogan, then you need not worry about any form of decoration; each person's entry will be read and judged on its own merit. Plain white paper and a normal white or manila envelope are all that you need to use – any extra effort will be a waste of your precious time.

A summary of plain paper entry techniques

- Interpret plain paper to mean a sheet of any single-colored paper unless the rules stipulate that you must use white only. Effective single colors include yellow, black, blue, green and anything fluorescent

- Use a wide-nibbed pen to write with (marker pens are ideal for this purpose). Use a contrasting colored ink to your paper

- Write your name and address details as large as possible, extending right to each edge of the paper

- Use fancy or childlike writing for best effect; remember, this writing style is normal for some people, so why shouldn't you do it too?

- Unless there is a size limit on the paper that you are allowed to submit, make it as large as you wish. Small pieces of paper are easily 'lost' within a large pile of entries

- Avoid any patterned paper (including lined paper) or fancy edging effects

- Enter several times if the rules allow you to, and try a different technique with each entry, including at least one entry that doesn't bend the rules in any way

- Use white paper and standard envelopes if you have to submit a slogan

Internet and Phone-in Contests

❝ I'm a great believer in luck, and I find the harder I work the more I have of it. **❞**

Thomas Jefferson

Chapter 4
Internet and Phone-in Contests

There are many pros and cons to online and phone-in competitions, ultimately the decision is yours to make. You never know, you might even have desires to join an online members-only competition forum or club. Irrespective of however much you choose to engage with modern technology as your media of preference, the tips and advice below will help you to enter these safely and securely, whilst also protecting your personal information from fraudulent users.

Protecting your personal details

Most people are wary of entering personal details online for very obvious reasons. Identity theft has been a major concern since the use of email and online transactions have become commonplace. Think though, what details are you willingly offering to competition organizers each time you submit a postal entry? The chances are that you have given your name, address, and possibly even your home phone number. The difference with entering this same information online is that it can be intercepted or easily used or sold on elsewhere; please be careful.

Use the promoter's website only

It would be advisable to enter competitions like these only through the promoter's company website, and limiting the information that you supply to the absolute minimum. Check the details of how and when you will be contacted if you win a prize, and also tick all the boxes which restrict the company from passing on your details to third party organizations.

Avoiding unwanted emails

Ideally, you should never use your personal home email address or a work-based email account to enter online-based competitions. Once your name has been added to an email mailing list, you are at an increased risk of being inundated with unwanted incoming emails. This can be annoying, problematic, and potentially quite costly if your internet connection is on a pay-as-you-go 'dial-up' tariff rather than an all-inclusive broadband contract.

It is incredibly easy to set up an additional email or webmail account (such as Hotmail) free of charge and it would be advisable for you to do so if you intend to enter online competitions on a regular basis. The advantage of a webmail or 'disposable' email account is that you can check your messages via a web server, and can delete them at source if you wish to do so without downloading them to your computer.

Advantages to you

Online website entries are quick and cheap, which is why many compers have started to use them. For the same cost of one postal entry, you could be online for several minutes if you have a 'pay-as-you-go' internet connection, allowing you to make five or six entries of the prize draw style of contest. For broadband internet users, the cost of entering online competitions is effectively free. Most compers see the low cost as an incentive to enter as many online competitions as possible, though there is a much lower chance of winning anything owing to the high number of

" If at first you don't succeed, cheat! **"**

Anon

entrants. One thing to beware of, apart from there being no skill element attached to winning these competitions, there is a likelihood of receiving an increased level of spam emails.

Lost in the post

Entries submitted online are not subject to postal delays or Post Office collection times. You will be assured that your entry has arrived on or before the deadline date once you hit the 'send' or 'submit' button.

Daily prizes

A few promoters are now offering daily prizes as an instant win type contest. Text addresses for these are often found on grocery item labels, soft drinks bottles and cans, or on confectionery wrappers. Entry is usually via a text message from your cell phone (you text a product code number which is unlikely to be 'unique') or via a web page. Postal entries might be offered, though I wouldn't rely on this option, owing to the inevitable time delay.

This generates a significant amount of repeat business for the competition promoter. Prize winners will be randomly selected. If you are planning on entering this type of competition, I suggest you target the end of the promotion period, when the large majority of other entrants will have lost interest, thus increasing your chance of success, albeit slightly.

Disadvantages

Once your details have been entered online via a website, they are permanently available to the competition promoters and this does pose a risk of interception or of being sold to third party operators. You are likely to be inundated with unwanted spam emails. There will be many more identical entries that you are competing against, and the selection will be random – you have no opportunity to influence the outcome.

Crafty Marketing

If your home phone number is in a telephone directory, the chances are you will be contacted at some stage by telesales marketing companies who sometimes use the tactic of informing you that you have won a cruise holiday, timeshare holiday home or a free trial of one of their products. If you don't remember entering that type of competition, chances are you didn't; it is likely to be a marketing scam. Likewise, if callers don't know your name (which they should do if you are a prize winner), don't give them any details – treat it as it is, a nuisance call.

Can the judge's decision be influenced?

The ability to influence a judge with internet competition submissions is extremely limited, unless you are permitted to send details by email rather than via a webpage entry form. With emails you can select font style, color and size, as well as providing background effects (wallpaper). Don't follow the crowd – make your entry garish, with large fonts and hideous colors, just in case all entries are printed out. You might be lucky, and have a prize awarded by this method, particularly if there is a dual submission route (post and online) as my local newspaper sometimes offers. If there is an alternative postal option, then your email will almost certainly be printed out and added to the pile, thus saving you a postage cost. I advise you to send an entry by both methods of submission (by post and email) if the rules permit it – you can never be sure whether multiple prizes are allocated across different submission routes.

Check if you can enter by post instead

Many competitions offer you the opportunity to enter by phone or via a website. These details will be displayed prominently. If you check the small print, there might be an opportunity to submit details by mail. Not everyone has access to an internet connection; others may have an ex-directory landline telephone.

Why are promoters offering this style of competition?

By offering an online competition via a website, the promoters have the opportunity to advertise their products to you. The cost of running an online competition is considerably cheaper for them than a major campaign involving printed media. You are responsible for paying the phone or internet charge to access the web page – the only cost to the promoter is the prize itself, and perhaps a member of staff's time associated with judging any slogans that have been submitted (depending on the style of the competition).

Phone-in and text-entry competitions

These really are best avoided. Often the questions that you need to answer are incredibly simple (producing a huge number of entries) and the cost of a phone call is high. You might well find that you are paying premium rate call charges. The call length will last for a minute or more and there will be an advertising message before you are able to register your answer to a question and enter your address. The cumulative cost of all compers' calls will be used to fund the reimbursement of the cost of any prize offered. Text entry competitions will usually be to a premium rate phone number, and may feature a return text which you might need to pay for, even though you have very little chance of winning a prize.

TV phone-ins

There has been a lot of controversy with phone-in competitions promoted by television programs, with several high-profile television companies recently having received very large financial penalties for abuse of the system. These competitions usually feature a simple question based on a program that you might just have watched, and attract a huge number of telephone callers to a premium-rate telephone number. Your chance of success is extremely slim. A winner will be chosen at random. You will possibly still be charged for your call even if you miss the entry deadline.

Writing Effective Slogans

“ If you can come up with a snappy little slogan, then you have a future in winning tagline competitions or being a political speech writer. **”**

Mark Hansen

Chapter 5
Writing Effective Slogans

Go on, admit it, you must be a teeny bit jealous of the compers who nab the big prizes. I used to think that too, but now I'm amongst those people whom I used to envy. Believe me, it's easier than you think to enter and win slogan competitions – hold your nerve, practice your technique and go for it! Soon the prizes should be arriving at your door.

Low entry rate

The competitions which receive the fewest entries will obviously offer you the best odds of winning; this is the case for tie-breaker slogans. If you talk with other people who occasionally enter prize draws, you will inevitably find that most of them will steer well clear of anything that requires a slogan, mainly because they don't think they have any chance of winning. So how do you learn to be a winner in this field? By practicing and making a few mistakes on the way…

I initially found slogans to be the biggest challenge, mainly because I didn't approach them with the right level of confidence. After hundreds of failed efforts using entries based on other people's winning slogans, I broke free from all restraints and developed my own method, which I hope works for you as well.

Keep it cheerful

When creating slogans it is always advisable to keep the tone of your text bright, cheerful and complimentary to the product or manufacturer (or both if you have a large word count to utilize). An uplifting mood, cleverly interspersed with topic-related words or puns is bound to attract the attention of the reader, and hopefully earn you the reward you seek. Whenever I have won a slogan tie-breaker prize, the response from the promoter has been that my slogan was amusing. Obviously, this will not always be the case, but it is an ideal place to start.

Writer's block

There will usually be a lead-in question to answer, or a phrase to complete with a limited number of extra words (between 10 and 15 words is about average). This doesn't sound too difficult so far does it? The problem arises when you sit down to complete the entry form, and suffer the familiar writer's block. There is no need to worry, it's quite normal – we all get this from time to time.

Keep your nerve

This unnecessary 'panic' is the stage at which most people give up and decide not to enter the competition at all, which is a bonus for the few of us who hold our nerve and spend a few hours (or even days) perfecting our written masterpieces. The prizes on offer for this type of competition are usually of a significant value, so take your time in perfecting your choice of slogan to enter; it should be worth your effort.

Is it worth the effort?

I'm proud to declare that I won a car from my local Safeway supermarket a few years ago, all for less than ten words on a piece of paper and a few hours spent assembling and perfecting my slogan. Eight thousand pounds worth of prize, all for less than a day's worth of effort. With confidence, patience, and a little practice, you could achieve this too.

Which slogans have won before?

A good place for you to start will be to look through the section on 'popular off-the-shelf slogans' to check the style of phrase that has swayed the judges in the past, and then modify one or two of the slogans for your own use. After a few attempts you will notice that as your technique improves, your confidence will begin to soar.

Take your time

Jot all your notes, thoughts and partial attempts for your tie-breaking slogan down on scrap paper or a dedicated note book. Take your time and let your ideas flow. It really is an exciting experience. Why not involve your family at this stage? Record all of their ideas, even the silly ones; it is possible that something might evolve from these. One word of warning though: do not be tempted to write anything on your entry form at this stage, as altered forms will definitely be discarded, and you will have wasted your time, effort and the opportunity to win your dream prize.

What will you need?

Equip yourself with a note pad, pencil and eraser so that you can jot down your thoughts as they spring to mind. I would also advise that you obtain a hard-backed note book in which you record the slogans that you actually submit for each competition, along with the closing date and details of which prizes are on offer. There is nothing more embarrassing than receiving a congratulatory phone-call informing you of your winning entry when you have forgotten ever having entered for it.

Re-use your winning slogans

If you win a prize, check which of your slogans brought you the success. This is easy if you only entered once, otherwise if possible, ask the organizer when you are contacted to make arrangements to deliver your prize. This will be invaluable information that you can use to your advantage again at a later date for a similar themed competition. Depending on the circumstances, you might even be able to re-use your slogan without having to change any of the wording. However it is good practice not to use other people's winning slogans without modifying them.

The cringe factor

When I look back at some of my early attempts I cringe! I am not at all surprised that they were overlooked; they were neither witty, rhyming, or product-specific. The benefit of reviewing your previous work is to convince yourself of the progress you have made, often in a relatively short period of time. Go on – have a giggle!

Different styles of slogan

There are several styles of slogan that are worth considering; it is worth having a go at all of them, especially since you do not know which style any particular judge will actually prefer (believe it or not, they're all human...).

1. The first letter of each word spells the name of a product, for example:

   PEPSI – **P**opular **E**ffervescing **P**otion **S**timulates **I**nterest

2. Adapt a standard 'off-the-shelf' slogan that has already won a similar prize

3. Use topic-specific puns, associated words, or rhymes to make your slogan amusing, for example: Watts an Ohm without a phone? (This has an electrical theme)

4. Combining the promoter's products with the prize theme

5. A short poem (for high word-count allowances)

PRIZE T!P

There are certain non-mentioned conventions that you must follow, to avoid instant rejection: avoid rudeness and political or racist remarks, flatter the promoter, and use correct grammar and spelling for the language you are entering in (i.e. UK and US English spellings). Anything else is fair play.

A worked example – producing a slogan

Consider a fictitious competition promoted between McEwan's export lager and the ASDA supermarket. Let's assume that the prize is a holiday in Scotland.

The lead-in phrase is: 'McEwan's export lager is perfect for a holiday in Scotland because...' which should be completed in ten words or fewer. We have everything that we need, so how do we get started? Firstly, take two or three tried and tested slogans from the popular off-the-shelf slogans list (holidays and drinks section) and try to adapt them.

Here are two suitable slogans to start with:

- '...Quality taste, classic bottle design, the label is <product name>, the pleasure is mine.' (13 words)

- '...The cream of creations shares the dream of locations.' (9 words)

The next step is to manipulate each slogan individually, to make them flow properly (if you pardon the pun) and to mention either the prize or the sponsor, or ideally both of them.

Starting with the first slogan, which exceeds the permitted word-count: '...Quality taste, classic design, the label is McEwan's, the pleasure is mine.'

This first attempt sounds too awkward when you read it aloud; it has the wrong rhythm, with too many syllables around the McEwan section. Now for a second attempt, integrating the prize destination this time: '...Quality taste, Scottish design, labelled McEwan, pleasure's all mine.'

This meets the word count and also mentions the prize, so it would be worth entering as one of your slogans.

The second slogan I chose is possibly a little more challenging, as there isn't a 'blank' to fill in with the sponsor or prize. You could try using it 'as is' or tailor it to suit your competition. The problem with using this slogan without any form of alteration is that the judging team could well have seen it before, and is therefore unlikely to select it as a winner. You could take a chance, submit it in its original form, and hope for the best, but ideally you need to make the slogan uniquely yours. So let's inject a little Scottish flavor to the beer: '…**This highland creation shares the dream of locations.**' It is a move in the right direction, but doesn't have the 'feel' of being a winning slogan just yet. One more minor change and we should see the final version taking shape, well within the ten-word maximum word count limit:

'…**This highland creation – a taste sensation.**' This could well be a winner and worthy of submission.

Rest with it a while

Don't be too hasty to mail your slogans, leave them a few days before you enter the competition. How annoyed would you be to discover that you could have 'fine-tuned' your slogan after you had already put it in the mailbox? An expensive prize is likely to be awarded to the most polished slogan submitted – make sure that yours is the very best that you are capable of producing. Keep a pad of paper handy and jot down variations of your slogan over a period of several days. Read your final versions to your family or friends to gain their opinions, after all, if the prize is for a holiday, they will probably hope to share it with you, so make them earn it!

Don't forget to include the qualifier

The time has come to send in your entry – if there is a qualifier receipt or label, don't forget to include it with your form (staple it on if necessary), otherwise your efforts have been wasted.

Keep within the limits

Apart from ensuring that your slogan meets the required maximum word-count limits, you must make sure that your writing fits within the allocated spaces on the entry form – this is really important. Practice writing your slogan out onto a separate piece of paper first, just to make sure that it is small enough to fit into the allocated area on the form. Use a pen with a fine-sized nib if possible (never use pencil). It will be hugely disappointing if your writing overlaps the edge of the slogan box on your form and your entry is rejected (especially if you have only managed to obtain one form).

Multiple entries

If you have the option of sending in more than one slogan, try to make them very different in their overall styles. Above all, aim to mail these off in plenty of time to meet the deadline date. If you are doubtful of the quality of your slogan and the deadline is looming, don't hang on to it, send your entry without further modification, or pick something straight from the list that I have provided; the odds of winning will always be better than not entering at all.

It is so easy to talk yourself out of entering, just like the majority of people who only dabble at entering competitions. Remember, the odds are in your favor, all you need to do is to submit something, and you're part way to success already.

Regular winners

There are many popular slogans that repeatedly win prizes, a few of which you might have come across before. A consideration in national competitions is that several people may use the same 'off-the-shelf' slogan as you, in which case all the duplicates are likely to be rejected – make sure that yours is not one of these, and adapt it slightly. Often just a slight modification to the phrasing of the slogan or the introduction of a pun or two is all that you need to earn merit with the judges.

PRIZE T!P

If you have been provided with a generous word-count limit, then why not use it to your advantage? A short, rhyming poem or limerick is considerably more likely to win a prize than a long explanation or waffle. You do not have to use the whole word-count allocation.

A few seconds is all you have

Judges will probably spend only a few seconds reading each entry, so keep your slogan short and snappy. If you have a restrictive word-count limit, then make up a few words, or where appropriate, try to hyphenate several of them.

PRIZE T!P

If you enter a slogan-based competition, there is often an option to send a stamped addressed envelope to the promoters after the closing date to obtain details of the winners and their entries. This is worth doing if you wish to enter similar competitions in the future.

Slogan essentials

- If you are new to writing slogans, it would be wise to start by selecting a tried and tested winning slogan from the 'popular off-the-shelf slogans' section and modify it to include the manufacturer, prize, or both

- Keep well within the word-count limit

- Hyphenate words if you need to (they only count as one word)

- Read your slogan aloud to check whether it rhymes or flows correctly.

- Select two or three variations of each of your slogans if you have time, and ask family or friends to comment on them

- Practice writing out your slogan on a separate piece of paper to ensure it will fit into the allocated space on the entry form. If you overlap the edges or make alterations on the form, your entry is likely to be disqualified

- Keep a pad, pencil and eraser handy to jot down any word associations or improvements to your slogan(s) as they spring to mind

- Keep a record of all the slogans you have submitted, along with the closing dates and the prizes that are offered with each competition. You might need to refer to this information at a later date

Popular off-the-shelf slogans (and a few of my own winners)

I have separated the list of popular slogans (a few of which are my own winning creations) into categories of suppliers and/or products, which I hope you will find helpful. There are a few that have a high cringe factor; however, they do seem to win frequently.

Find a style that you are comfortable with, and use these templates to create something unique, and success will not be far off for you. As I have mentioned before, if you keep a record of each entry you send in, you'll soon establish which styles certain promoters are seeking. You will also be able to look back through your records and select those phrases that could be further improved, until you have your own personalized selection of special slogans that can be used to dazzle the judging panels, whatever the prize might be.

Adhesives and DIY theme

- It creates a bond so unique, extremely strong, never weak
- A small deposit secures any article
- Its name is its bond
- It's being reliable that makes it buyable
- Experts perfect it, professionals select it

Bike theme

- The taste brings satisfaction, replacing thirst with five-speed action
- I prefer mountain bikes to mounting bills

Booze theme

- It satisfies the guys, and quenches the wenches

- Perfect quality is superbly presented, leaving palate pleased, and pockets contented

- Candle-lit supper? Family invasion? <supplier>'s <product name> makes the occasion

- It's the distinguished label for the festive table

- Superior cognac, delivered by Santa, satisfies the discerning decanter

- Sipping <product name> makes Christmas very jolly, for Carol, Ivy, Noel and Holly

- Quality taste, classic bottle design, the label is <product name>, the pleasure is mine

- It's straight from the stills, and still the best straight

- It's the ruler by which other beers are measured

- Pampers the palate, mellows the mood, it's beautifully creamy, and expertly brewed

- They're two of the finest things to come from Cannes

- Every opening is a premier occasion

- After a long day, I sip into something special

- When the cork pops out, my friends pop in

- Experts perfect it, connoisseurs select it

- It's in a glass of its own

- It's thirst come, thirst served

Carpet theme

- Always home grown, dyed and spun, copied by many, bettered by none

Car theme

- Stylish, handsome, safe and true, if only <manufacturer> made men too!

- It's supercoloredfuturisticmaxiairyspacious

- Every special outing deserves an inner treat

- Powerful flavor, dynamic display, stunning performance, drive of the day

- Winning wheels, heavenly brew, teamed together, a dream come true

- They motivate this lumpy lassie to gain herself a classy chassis

- For flavor and style, it wins by a mile

- A leader in its class, a formula one cannot surpass

- Exhilaration and zest make this cabriolet my quest

Cheese theme

- It takes the biscuit

- It's the star onboard, with port aside

- Don't rely on cupid's dart, serve heavenly cheese, and win his heart

Electrical theme

- Dim is what I used to be, until <manufacturer name> bulbs enlightened me

- Watts an Ohm without one?

- For <product> or <product> they know Watt's what!

- It's the cell of the century

- It sells fast because its cells last

- An enduring reputation guarantees an electrifying performance

Fantasy theme

- To be Cleopatra, and let Julius Caesar

- Cakes look great with candles lit, make a wish – this is it!

Fish theme

- Superior quality tips the scales, other brands just fisherman's tales

- Superior fish, outstanding taste, kind to pocket, heart and waist

- Quality fish, a Scottish tradition, provides a meal with healthy nutrition

- For healthy living, there is no doubt, nothing beats a Scottish trout

Food (general) theme

- Heard on the grapevine, they are best, tried and tested, most impressed

- Nothing gets eaten fasta than <manufacturer name> pasta

- It's the after dinner guest that speaks for itself

- Every biteful's delightful

- There's gold in them there jars

- For quality, value, taste and tradition <product name> defies competition

- They're made by wizards, eaten by goblins

- <Product>'s taste is its crowning glory, <producer>'s fringe benefits complete the story

- There's no need to be hasty, with something this tasty

- I'm on a roll of anticipation

- <Product name> crosses the line – beyond delicious to divine

- It tops off the menu, whatever the venue

- One good churn deserves another

- Action packed, full of taste, <product> meals mean no waste

- Their name is on everyone's lips

- To be specific – it tastes terrific

Fruit and preserves theme

- They're the apple of my mother's eye

- One good name preserves another

Gardening theme

- Seasons come, seasons go, < supplier>'s seeds will always grow

- What Edison made for duty <flower bulb brand> perfected for beauty

- Quality seeds I adore, fork out less, rake in more

General theme

- I always say hello to good-buys

- Having discovered perfection, why risk random selection?

- <Producer> expertise, <shop> pricing, makes <product> unbeatably enticing

Hair products theme

- Radical style with fringe benefits

- For control and style, it wins by a mile

- It sparks the flair into your hair

- The perfect head start

- It gives you the style to get you noticed

- A lifetime devoted to innovation…who better to style the new generation

- Drab, frumpy, overweight; new hairstyle will rejuvenate

Health foods and health products theme

- Getting near my sell-by-date, <product name> helps me to rejuvenate

- Light, tasty, full of vits, smoothes away my lumpy bits

- It plays a part in protecting your heart

- If tickers could talk, they'd sing for this tucker

- It tastes absolutely flabulous

- It's the way to indulge, whilst beating the bulge

- <manufacturer name> takes the view – indulgence should be healthy too

- 100% taste, nothing to waist

- It's the <product name> that re-45s me

- Delicious on the lips – murder on the hips

Holiday theme

- The cost is nominal, the fun phenomenal

- Nearer than you think, when you take the Chunnel link

- The cream of creations shares the dream of locations

- I've got the guide, I know the phrases, thanks to <promoter name> I'm going places

- If the world's your oyster, then <place name>'s the pearl

- A dream come true, thanks to you

Meats and barbecues theme

- They are leg and shoulders above the rest

- It's sheer perfection

- It's always the shoulder to rely on

- Lamb reared and prepared by master, prevents 'lamb on table' disaster

- <Product> guarantees a hot reception, flaming good value without exception

- Succulence and flavor in every slice, quick and easy, everyday price

- Wholesome, fun, delicious too, they're always on the barbecue

- Just a little grilling reveals all its juicy secrets

- It's the porc-u-pine for

Soft drinks theme

- It's refreshingly cool, stunningly chic, the style and taste, together unique

- It's luscious, invigorating, provocative, and sensual

- As Brutus declared to Julius Caesar, it's a phara-old treat for a thirsty Giza!

- Heaven is only a ring pull away

- Whenever friends gather and mingle, <drink name> provides the tingle

- It reigns where it pours

Spices and flavorings theme

- The spice is right

- Coolest taste, hottest flavor, at <shop name>'s price, a money saver

- This money saver is full of flavor

- It has the flavor my taste buds love to savor

Miscellaneous themes

- A pioneering quest to deliver the best

- It's the perfect home for a gastronome

- Once tried, you'll never change

- It's nifty and neat, it works like a treat

- We know what we like, and we like what we trust

- The quality's terrific, the effect stunning, a perfect addition to female cunning

- Past experience makes the perfect present

- The best things in life are sugar free, as every tooth fairy will agree

- Both are designed with the other in mind

- Traditional values, built on fun; a reputation second-to-none

A flash of inspiration?

After a while, you'll find writing slogans comes quite naturally to you and occasionally you'll pen something absolutely sensational without having a competition to focus on; a true flash of inspiration. If you can think of a company who might be thrilled to use it as an advertising slogan, why not send it to them with a gushing cover note about why you've always liked their products? Chances are they'll send you something as a reward for your effort. It is worth a try.

Competitors' magazines and online resources

If you are just beginning the process of entering consumer competitions, then you might wish to subscribe to a monthly competitors' magazine such as *Competitors Companion.* Most serious competitors will have heard of this and other useful magazines at some stage in their 'comping career', and have found them to be a useful source of slogans that have won recent competitions. Try to obtain a sample copy before you sign up to a lengthy subscription, as per all magazines.

Judges follow fashion

Just like clothing trends, judges who sit on panels to select slogan winners follow fashions – advertising fashion trends. What was popular last year might not be this year's 'in' theme, so do keep an eye on the styles of slogans that are winning the major competitions, as well as any 'cool and trendy' phrases that are in current use. Add them to your essential slogan list and try to mimic them with one of your spare entries.

Steal or borrow

Someone else's luck could be your good fortune with the next competition. If you spot a clever slogan in a competition or in an advertisement, jot it down, modify it, and re-use it to your advantage. We're all told to do our bit for recycling, aren't we? Don't be too proud to borrow a phrase or two, especially if you are submitting more than one slogan for a competition.

Seriously humorous

You know nothing about the judge's preference. I advise sending up to three slogans per competition for the really valuable prizes: one humorous, one gushingly flattering, and one which is seriously sensible (but definitely not boring).

Duplicates

No matter which style of slogan you choose, the judge must be convinced that it is original. You don't have to assume that he or she has had access to the publicized winning entries to other competitions, but be sensible. A winning entry for the same company for a previous year's competition will not be selected again. Duplicated entries (from several competitors) will be noticed, especially at the final selection stage, and will be discarded.

PRIZE T!P

If you enter a poem for a large word count slogan competition, make sure it rhymes and is witty; above all, keep it simple. Modern poetry formats do not lend themselves to this type of competition.

Target a restaurant with a poem

There are several big events in every hotel or restaurant owner's promotional brochure, each of which relies on testimonials from satisfied customers. Be brave and contact a few in writing, asking if they are running any competitions to win a wedding event, birthday party, valentines' evening meal or a Christmas dinner for a group of friends.

Send the manager a hand-written copy of a poem written specially for his or her restaurant and offer it as a satisfied customer's testimonial (look at the menu and create something appropriate, even if you've never been there before… lie if you need to!). Remember – the art of manipulation is a skill you will develop as you become more and more successful with this hobby.

For the sake of a quick poem and a postage stamp, the chances are that you'll earn yourself a meal out for two people or more and the venue might consider a competition in conjunction with the local newspaper (probably for the lesser value of the options you gave). Free advertising for them and a meal out for you; everyone's a winner.

Poetry and short story competitions

I have included these two competition types in this section because they will attract slogan writers – poetry competitions are quite a natural progression for those people who think in rhymes. There is a knack to it, though this is not to say that poetry is at all simple – far from it. Poets can easily apply their technique to crafting a perfect slogan.

Competition details for poetry and short story competitions are usually announced several months in advance. A good place to look for them is in writers' magazines and on publishers' websites. There are a few writing competition newsletters and online resources that you can access, for example, *Kudos magazine*, *Writers News* and *Prize Magic*. Alternatively, an internet search for 'writing competitions' will provide you with plentiful options.

Research the judges

Writing competitions almost always have a prominent writer or poet as the judge or there may be a panel of judges, the names of whom are given in the promotional material. This gives you an advantage in that you can research each of their published work and style preferences. Use this information wisely and write your poem or story in a suitable style. For example, if you know the judge is a stickler for grammar and detests contemporary poetry formats, ensure your work is punctuated correctly and aim to produce work which cannot be confused with anything other than a traditional poetry form. If the judge is an editor for a specific publishing house, find out what the normal submission guidelines are and submit work that meets the publisher's own 'house style'.

Reading fees

Poetry competitions, along with short story competitions, attract a huge number of entries from skilled writers, however, that does not mean that you should steer clear of these. The downside is that you will need to pay a fee to enter the competition – this is a 'reading fee'. Think how much longer a two-thousand word essay takes to read compared with a ten-word slogan! Do not enter if this fee is more than one tenth of the cash value that is awarded to the winner. There are a few competitions that sport prizes well in excess of $1,000 – look out for them.

Unpublished poets and authors

A few competitions in this category are limited to unpublished entrants only. Beware that 'published' also means any work that has appeared in newspapers or on websites. This applies to poems, stories, articles and e-novels. It is not taken to mean blogs or other non-literary work (which applies to most of us in this technological era).

Protecting your copyright

Read the competition small print very carefully for writing competitions. Novice writers may not be aware that anything you have written is your copyright. A few competitions will require you to assign copyright of the work to the organizers, even if you are not a main prize winner – if you see this, I suggest you avoid entering. Once you have assigned the copyright to someone else, you can never have that work published elsewhere – it is no longer yours. It is a trap many novice writers fall into. Remember – if you are a prize winner, and your work is due to be published online, in a magazine or perhaps a book, the only rights you should consider assigning to the publisher are your publishing rights, not copyright. If in doubt, don't enter.

Sharing Your Hobby

66 A quitter never wins and a winner never quits. **99**

Napolean Hill

Chapter 6
Sharing Your Hobby

There's a real feel-good sensation when your efforts are complimented and appreciated by the people you care about. Friends and family can be useful to you in all sorts of ways; find out how in this chapter, and use it to everyone's advantage.

Anticomperitis

At some stage you will probably encounter a few friends or members of your family who ridicule your new hobby, possibly out of jealousy or lack of skills on their own behalf – this is commonly referred to as 'anticomperitis'. This strange phenomenon will almost certainly reverse following your first few wins. My husband used to suffer from this ailment whenever I asked him to drop my hideously-decorated home-made postcard entries into the local post box; his embarrassment obviously got the better of him. If this happens to you, rest assured that there is a cure – it's amazing what a few big wins can do to pep up the enthusiasm of family members.

Sharing success

It might take a while, but eventually your family and friends will take your new-found hobby seriously, demonstrated by the excitement they show at the prospect of sharing your various rewards with you. They will soon begin to look forward to receiving the regular free meals out, theme park tickets, and other treats that they wouldn't normally be able to afford, all at the expense of your goodwill and effort.

Most compers enjoy sharing their success with their friends; after all, it's the thrill of winning that drives the compulsion to enter competitions rather than the need for the prize itself.

Spare places?

You will find that there are many competitions that offer prizes of family tickets, meals for four or more people, birthday parties, pamper days; the list is endless. The problem arises when your own family set-up does not have the correct number of people to fulfil the prize requirements, your children are too young to leave alone with babysitters for a few nights, or your partner is away on business. In such cases, you should attempt to fill the place with friends or other relatives to avoid appearing rude to the competition organizers (for example, two people occupying a table for six in a restaurant will appear disrespectful to the host).

A rota for friends

The competition details might even require you to forfeit the prize (which is rarely seen) if you do not meet the original terms and conditions of the prize offer. The question is, who will you choose to accompany you, whilst avoiding squabbles between friends and accusations of favoritism? The best option is to draw up an unofficial rota for your friends, thereby causing the least offence. This goodwill gesture of a free shared prize is normally accepted readily.

My earliest competition memories

Family and friends always support the achievements of people they care about, and this encourages further effort and continuing success; my family were no different to me when I first started entering competitions as a school girl. It came as no surprise to my parents that I gained notoriety as a prize-winning artist – of coloring competitions! When I was about ten years old, I won the first of many coloring competitions which featured in my local newspaper. The competitions usually appeared at around

Christmas time and coincided with the pantomime at the town theatre, which provided the theme for the competition. The winning entries were all displayed on a notice board outside the theatre for the whole duration of the pantomime performances. I soon became a talking point amongst my friends, and it certainly did no harm to my self-esteem as an artist at school. Without their support, I doubt that my winning streak would have continued for so long.

Unwanted recognition

Until a few years ago there was a regular children's feature page in the local paper to color in a picture and win a book. Embarrassingly, my young son won it nearly every time he entered. I say embarrassing merely because a photographer arrived at our house after every win, so that they had a photo of my son to use in the newspaper. After each win we 'rested' for a few weeks to give other local children a chance to win something, and for it not to appear too obvious that my child was greedily hogging all of the prizes. Eventually our winning streak was foiled – one of the many photographers that had been to our house recognized the child and location from previous visits, and asked the obvious question "Haven't I been here before?" This was the last time the weekly competition appeared in the paper. We had a good run whilst it lasted.

PRIZE T!P
KEEPING YOUR FRIENDS INFORMED
One way to keep the euphoria of winning something alive is to tell people about it. Even the little wins are special. I phone my friends regularly with updates, and they do the same with their wins – it keeps the enthusiasm going for all of us.

Going head-to-head

I tend not to enter the same competitions that I am aware my friends have entered for, particularly the local ones if the number of prizes on offer are very restricted. I consider it to be inappropriate, since I win such a high proportion of what I enter for. There have been several occasions when we have won all of the prizes on offer for particular competitions.

Helping new compers

I occasionally have requests for help from purchasers of my first published book, Competitive Edge: Prize Winning Secrets. I actually find this quite flattering, and have usually assisted when my work schedule allows. It is reassuring, and a huge boost of confidence, to know that you have assisted another new comper to become a successful prize winner. I consider that, as the popularity of this hobby grows, especially in the current 'difficult' world economic climate, more company advertising promotions will follow the competition route because of their cheap implementation. By encouraging more people to enter competitions because of the wonderful array of prizes on offer, we are all promoting the benefits of this form of advertising to the competition sponsors. Does this make sense to you? I do hope so.

Slogan workshop

After a while, as your slogan-writing expertise develops, you will start to receive requests from friends and family who would also like to win something special. Believe me, this really does happen; their attempts will probably be amusingly poor, but you'll feel compelled to help. By all means, guide them in the right direction, and support their enthusiasm. If they show a real interest in this hobby, I would be inclined to encourage them further by spending time working with them to write simple slogans which can be used to enter their choice of competition. Compers often work in isolation – to have a few friends to share ideas with is a bonus. You might even find that after a few attempts at writing slogans theirs could be better placed in the prize rankings than yours, in which case, congratulations are in order.

It's the thought that counts

During my short spell as a secondary school teacher, my pupils (knowing of my car, cash and holiday successes) would regularly hand me scribbled slogans that I could 'try using for the next prize'. I found their display of support for me quite sweet in a way, though their written offerings were often not as appropriately phrased as I would have liked.

Clubs

There are a few competitor clubs around, but these are few and far between. There are several online members' clubs in which you can give and receive advice, as well as find details of forthcoming competitions. The drawback of this is that everyone chases the same prizes. Why not do an internet search and see what you can find?

Ask friends for help

It is likely that your close friends have another outer circle of friends, all of whom can be of assistance to you. If you are looking for competitions on a certain theme, for example you need a new fridge/freezer, why not ask around for entry forms or competition details? You will find that help floods in as soon as your successful reputation becomes common knowledge, especially after you have shared a few prize treats with them.

Swap entry forms

I regularly receive envelopes containing entry forms in the post from my comping friends, and dutifully return spares of anything that I have collected. I never know what I'm about to receive, which makes the entries more exciting. My preference for slogan competitions is well known amongst my friends, so they set me a challenge which I find hard to resist. Try it yourself. If you win a prize that you don't really want by this method, then you can safely assume that the person who sent you the original entry form might be an appropriate recipient of it.

Win to order

I have no qualms about entering competitions for other people (with their permission), as long as they supply me with the postage stamps and the competition details.

Making gifts of unwanted prizes

We all do it – win stuff we don't remember entering for. These make excellent presents for unsuspecting (and sometimes ungrateful, non-amused) friends and family. I have a box full waiting for a suitable recipient.

I know that I have been on the receiving end of a few similar prizes that my friends have won – things that I know they wouldn't normally have bought. One example of this is a pair of shoes which were one size too small for me...

Taking another winner's place

Occasionally compers 'swap' prizes or trade places by consent. It's always a surprise to find out what special arrangements or celebrations have been laid on for the 'real' winner when you get to the venue to accept the prize. Keep up the pretence, and take what comes your way graciously, and you can be assured of a memorable occasion. It can be highly amusing at the time, and hilarious for months afterwards when retelling the story to other people. If you accept a prize in place of somebody else, then please make sure you take some form of non-photographic identification with you – often the original prize winner's letter is all that is required. Check what type of identification a venue will accept before you go. Remember, most prizes stipulate that they are non-transferable, in which case, please adhere to the rules.

Selling unwanted prizes

Tickets for events that I subsequently find that I cannot attend for whatever reason, or other unusual items that will never be used are always offered to my friends and family first (free of charge). If they remain unwanted, they are promptly offered for sale on a well-known online auction site.

Winning for monetary value

There are a few prizes that you might target purely for their resale value. These might include theater tickets, limited edition CDs etc. If you find suitable competitions with high value prizes, this is an easy way to earn money which can then be used to fund your comping hobby.

Chasing the Big Wins

66 They gave me away as a prize once – a Win Tony Curtis For A Weekend competition. The woman who won was disappointed. She'd hoped for a second prize – a new stove. **99**

Tony Curtis

Chapter 7
Chasing the Big Wins

The perks of comping are numerous. Before long, you could join the elite group of winners who have experienced tailor-made events that are beyond your wildest dreams, as well as those high value prizes that you wouldn't normally be able to afford on the family budget. Set your target high, and rise to the challenge.

Especially for you

It is reassuring to think that in this age of excess, material possessions and high salaries, there are still a few experiences that simply cannot be bought. These are the one-off experiences and special events that the promoters stage especially for you. They can be 'behind-the-scenes' tours and activities, elaborately tailored excursions, opening events, naming celestial stars, spending time with your favorite celebrity, in fact anything that you could only ever dream of doing or becoming.

Beyond monetary value

Organizing this type of prize experience is a 'one off' event, and is likely to attract a great deal of publicity for the competition promoter. It will also involve an incredible amount of effort from a large number of people within the organization – this is beyond monetary value. If you are lucky (or skilful) enough to win an experience of this nature, you will have memories that stay with you forever. Savor every moment.

Give something back

It is likely that a slogan will be required for this type of high-value prize, along with your consent and willingness to take part in publicity photos, newspaper or radio interviews.

If the prize-giving ceremony is not subject to publicity, then the promoter will have missed out on a huge advertising opportunity. This doesn't happen too often. You need to consider that 'one-off-experience' style prizes are costly in terms of manpower and effort, therefore you must be prepared to give something back to the company in terms of your time and enthusiasm, if requested.

Take your camera

One thing that many people forget is to take their own camera, a spare set of batteries for it, and a memory card that has sufficient memory to capture those precious images and memories. Don't be too shy to ask a member of staff to take photos of you when you are actively involved in the activity, after all, it's your special day – enjoy it! These will be wonderful mementos to frame and display somewhere prominently in your home, and furthermore, they'll be a great inspiration to you if you ever hit a low spot with your winnings.

PRIZE T!P
SHOW YOUR APPRECIATION
Remember to send a thank you letter to the organizers after each big win – it's the very least you can do. It could encourage them to re-stage a similar event in the future for the benefit of other potential winners.

Contact your local newspaper

If the local newspaper hasn't covered the event in a feature, they would probably appreciate a photo of you with your prize and a few words relating to it. Blow your own trumpet once in a while – get your success publicized by sending a press release to the newspaper features editor. The facts are more likely to be correct if you have worded the article yourself. Graciously accept all the praise you are offered when friends and family phone to tell you they've seen a write-up relating to you.

Promises, promises

You've had your congratulations, and your name has been listed as the prize winner, well done! The problem arises when you have not received your prize – what do you do? If after a couple of weeks you have not received anything in the post, or have not received a collection request, then you need to chase up on the elusive prize. A quick courteous telephone call to the person who has signed the letter will produce the desired reaction; you might even be further compensated for the delay. Things do occasionally go missing in the postal system, and it might have already been dispatched in good faith.

Tickets that arrive too late

This is an awkward and frustrating problem if you have won tickets to an event and they have arrived too late for you to take advantage of them. Contact the organizer by telephone or email urgently – don't sit at home and simmer with anger about it. The result of your contact will probably be an alternative prize of equal value – be gracious in your negotiations and accept the outcome; after all, anything you receive will have been gained free of charge. You will not be offered a cash compensation. If the replacement tickets do not fit in with your social schedule, pass them onto somebody else (or sell them if there is time to do so).

Coke break – winning a much-needed holiday

Suffering from near total exhaustion, I knew that I needed time away from my demanding toddler, I needed a holiday! Paying for it wasn't really an issue, but I resented having to do so, especially since competition organizers have holiday prizes to give away and I had confidence in my

slogan skills. Other people win holidays, so why shouldn't I? I set mysei.
challenge of winning one for myself (and for my husband, of course) – I
was focused on a mission with no contingency for failure.

Spreading the word

I made it known to my friends that I needed a holiday and hoped they
would guide me in the direction of any holiday competition leaflets that
I hadn't already come across. It wasn't long before one of them (a fellow
competition enthusiast) visited me, clutching a spare entry form for a
weekend away courtesy of Diet Coke. She had only managed to obtain
two forms; one she gave to me, the other she kept for herself.

In general, I try not to enter head-to-head with my friends in competitions,
but I made an exception in this case – she obviously didn't mind the
challenge, else she wouldn't have given the form to me.

The task

To win the first prize, a holiday for two people, I needed to complete a
slogan in less than ten additional words. The slogan lead-in was: 'Drinking
Diet Coke is the ideal break from work because…'

This all seemed easy enough, but it had to be right first time, as I was
limited to one entry only. I set about focusing on what sort of people drink
Diet Coke, rather than the original variety, and why I would like to drink it;
I worked on the concepts of good taste, and it not being fattening. After
about an hour I knew deep down that I couldn't perfect the slogan further,
and posted my entry quickly, before I altered it again. The deadline was for
the next week, so I didn't have time to spend dwelling on it further.

The result

My winning slogan was: 'Drinking Diet Coke is the ideal break from work
because …it's 100% taste, with nothing to waist.'

A holiday gained for the price of a first class stamp and one hour's work – what a perfect, much-needed result.

I have seen my slogan used a few times since, which is an odd sensation; it obviously works, though other entrants have clearly plagiarized my work. If you're stuck for a suitable slogan for a diet drink then by all means, you are welcome to modify and re-cycle it for your own purpose. If I can do it, so can you.

Holidays during school term-time/semester

Holidays that are promoted as prizes are seldom likely to fit in with school holiday periods, when the peak season is in full swing. You will be offered specific time periods within which to take your break. Don't be put off by this, unless your children (if you have any) are in their main exam years. A carefully phrased letter to the head teacher with an explanation that the holiday is a prize will usually grant you approval to take the child out of school. A good idea would be to photocopy the prize letter as well, as proof to support your request. Do ensure that you have made a commitment for your children to take school work with them, so that they do not miss valuable curriculum time. Beware though, such a request is not automatically granted, so do not accept the prize until you have the school approval first.

An unusual experience – becoming a circus clown

Imagine how difficult it must be when you have just changed school, mid-way through the school year, and do not have your familiar group of friends to hang out with. My son found himself with this situation thrust upon him. How could I help him settle in? Throw a party of course!

I had seen a competition in the local newspaper to win the opportunity for one child to 'become a clown for the day', which coincided with Zippo's circus visiting our town. The prize included ten guests and ringside seating – the perfect excuse to invite eight new classmates, and two adult chaperones.

Big, bright and colorful postcard-entries

The competition to become a circus clown was a prize draw, and was highly likely to attract a huge number of entries from keen parents seeking family entertainment. I chose large, bright, hand-decorated postcards to send in; five entries in total to improve my odds of winning. Rather than commercial postcards, these were enormous hand-made ones, that couldn't possibly be missed in the post bag.

Obtaining consent

I obtained my son's consent to enter his name as the sender (this is essential if you are entering on somebody else's behalf), and briefed him on the answer to the qualifier question (in case he was asked about it at a later stage). All of the postcards were posted individually, each of them one day apart to ensure they were evenly distributed in the judge's pile.

Quick contact

I wrote my home daytime telephone number onto the card, so that I could receive a quick response if we won the prize, and to prevent the sponsors from having to waste time sending out a letter. Sure enough, the congratulatory phone call arrived on the afternoon that the draw was due to be held, and the booking was confirmed. Circuses are only in town for about a week, so all arrangements need to be made very swiftly.

Audience participation

The circus was certainly a memorable party which was thoroughly enjoyed by all of those who were not 'randomly' picked on to perform during the acts (only joking – they all had a great time, even my husband and another of our friends who had to dress up as a member of YMCA and dance!).

A year's supply of teabags

Sometimes, competitions are entered as a joke and the Twinings teabags competition was no exception to this notion when I noticed it in a local advertising newspaper. The competition was embedded within an advert for Twinings teas. The prize was a year's supply of their speciality tea in return for a suitably worded slogan. All I had to do was say why I wanted to win the prize (I actually detest the taste of tea!) in less than 30 words. There were no other guidelines – in my mind, it couldn't be more simple. Unusually though, the advert did not include any details of where to send the entry or when the closing date was; these omissions would certainly have put most people off entering. The odds were already in my favor – this was a challenge too good to resist; the prize was destined to be a surprise gift for my husband and son.

The tea-praising slogan

What did I write as my reason for wanting to win the prize? "I'd bungee jump from Heaven, or swim the seven seas, for the opportunity to sample all that tea!" None of which was further from the truth, but hey, I had a prize to win. I was determined that the prize would be mine. I thought this was worth the cost of a first class postage stamp, and hoped the judges would favor it. I had nothing to lose, and time was running short.

Imagine my surprise when I (a tea-hater) received the phone call to say I had won more than a thousand teabags. My family was delighted and extremely excited (which surprised me further); apparently it was just what they wanted!

Collecting the prize – careful timing

The only drawback to entering newspaper competitions is that you sometimes have to collect your prize rather than having it delivered – this happened to me on this occasion. The offices were only a fifteen-minute drive away, so I timed my visit carefully as I dreaded being offered a cup of

the celebrated tea and wouldn't have the nerve to decline it. To avoid this, I planned to arrive just before their lunch break – I hoped they would all be too keen to get rid of me quickly (hence no drink offer), so that they could go to lunch instead.

Ask the obvious

Admit it – you'd want to know why your slogan was better than the others, wouldn't you? Whilst in the office I just had to find out the answer to this question. I was amazed that over five hundred people had tried to win my prize, and that a lot of the entries were "not worth bothering with", which confirmed my suspicions that most people do not plan their tie-breakers carefully.

PRIZE T!P
FAILING TO PREPARE
It certainly pays to sit down and focus on your reasons for wanting to win a particular prize. A well-known phrase sums this up perfectly: 'If you fail to prepare, be prepared to fail.'

Do you want to party?

I cannot remember the last time that I had to pay for a party. There is a standing joke in my family that if you're looking for a good (but cheap) night out, then it's always best to "Ask Karen, and she'll win it for you!" This is a reputation that isn't always easy to live up to, after all, there has to be a prize available to win in the first instance.

Special occasions

Fortunately, there are plenty of competitions featured around specific annual celebration days and festive periods such as Christmas time, Valentine's Day and Mother's Day. Many of these are local competitions, and consequently will not have a huge number of entries. This is your opportunity to seek out parties and evening events. Look for competition details in your favorite pubs, clubs and newspapers.

Publicity at the venue – dress to impress

Be prepared to take part in publicity for the venue – it is a small price to pay for a free night's entertainment, which could be worth hundreds of pounds to you and your friends. You might find that a newspaper reporter or photographer (it is sometimes a dual role) has been booked, or that a member of the management team would like a quote from you and a photo for an in-house newsletter. Advice – go smartly dressed for the occasion in readiness for such a request.

Behave respectfully

As with all things in life, there are unwritten rules of behavior that you are expected to know and adhere to; this applies also when you are the star of an event, the main prize winner. The chances are that a lot of people will have been involved in making your day/evening a special occasion: you are a guest and must accept their hospitality gracefully and gratefully.

Getting drunk and disorderly just because the champagne is free-flowing is never acceptable; the same can be said for causing arguments and littering your conversation with profanities. You will bring shame on the organizers. It is better to remain sober, grit your teeth and say nothing, even if something doesn't quite meet with your approval. If the event is absolutely awful and you feel you really cannot stay a minute longer then I suggest you quietly pretend to look upset as you 'respond' to someone on your cell phone, then find and thank your hosts (if possible) as you leave for 'a family emergency' or something similar.

Repeat performance

My family and friends have helped to make up guest numbers for numerous meals out, ten-pin bowling events, birthday parties, private

"Winning is everything. The only ones who remember you when you come second are your wife and your dog."

Damon Hill

cinema screenings, theater performances and Christmas parties. I have even won tickets for the same bowling event for several years now, without raising suspicion from the organizers (though I expect that will all change if they read this book…).

Multiple birthday parties

It is a surprise to me how many 'birthday' parties my son can cram into a year – though his friends don't seem to object to attending this free entertainment. They have been well trained to avoid answering questions on the subject at the appropriate time – their compliancy suggests that they obviously recognize the benefits of the deal. The idea of keeping between 10 and 20 young children or teenagers amused for several hours on a weekend afternoon has earned me many reciprocal favors, and is certainly worth the effort of writing out several postcard entries and walking to the local post box (even in heavy rain!). The overall cost of the prize treat is minimal (stamps, postcards and invitations) whereas the peace and tranquillity at home is treasured and priceless. Try it, and don't be ashamed to book umpteen 'late' birthday parties throughout the year, when the opportunity arises.

Window mannequins

By far the oddest night out was the use of a private room for a Christmas party for up to twenty of my friends at my local Chicago Rock pub. With food, drink and music provided, this should have been a great night out – unfortunately, I couldn't mobilize twenty friends on a Friday evening at such short notice; there were only ten of us. We arrived in dribs and drabs, and were individually guided to our party room, which was a former shop window area – embarrassingly, we found ourselves on display to all the people passing by in the street! I always said that compers often have access to experiences that money can't buy. Being a shop mannequin for the evening wasn't quite what I had envisaged, but it can definitely be classed as the funniest and the most memorable so far. There will be many more, I'm sure.

Tips for parties

- Look in the local press, pubs and clubs for party competitions in the month running up to special occasions such as Christmas, Valentine's Day and Mother's Day

- Children's birthday party competitions are often offered if a venue is refurbished or gains new facilities. Enter for these at any time of the year, as a 'belated' birthday party if necessary – your child will be popular with his or her friends for months afterwards

- Organize a willing rota of friends that can be available at short notice to help you by filling your guest places for any 'evening-out' prizes that you might win. This might also be a useful incentive/reward for short-notice 'baby-sitting' services if you have a young child to look after

- Always write a thankyou letter to the proprietor of the venue of the prize you have received, and highlight any particularly good service you have experienced. Your courtesy might ensure that a similar competition is offered again in the future

- Dress appropriately for publicity photos

My most unusual prize – popsicles, popsicles and more popsicles

The very first article in a theater-focused magazine caught my attention – it was for a competition to win a popsicle every day for a year. What a bizarre prize! The fact that it was in an in-house magazine which wouldn't be read by anyone outside of a theater venue meant that there would be very few entries sent in. My imagination ran wild with unanswered questions, such as: How would I collect my prize? Would it be vouchers? Would I need to collect the popsicles from a specific shop? There were a lot of unanswered questions, and besides that, there wasn't even a competition closing date listed. Nevertheless, I rose to the bait, and sent in a postcard entry as soon as I got home.

A couple of weeks passed, and then a long white envelope slipped through my letterbox from the sponsors, Wall's Ice Cream. Unbelievably, I had actually won this unusual prize. My success did not meet with the usual enthusiasm from my family – they were deadly silent for a change.

A cool delivery

The letter requested that I phoned the supplier's order department to arrange delivery of my prize. There was one problem… the entire year's worth of popsicles would be delivered in one shipment, and they would arrive during the next week! Panic! Where would I store them? I had a very small fridge-freezer in my kitchen, which was already full. Accepting this delivery was beginning to become a logistical nightmare. Phone calls to all of my family and friends were rapidly made, so that all of the popsicles could be accommodated. I would receive the delivery of over 400 frozen packets, and have to distribute them all very quickly, before they melted.

I can see the funny side of this now, but am also a little more careful with the type of competition that I enter for. Don't put yourself in the same predicament as I found myself in – ensure that you are capable of accepting the delivery of each prize before you submit the competition entry.

Winning a car – the process I used

I'm sure you've heard it all before: "It's a fix!" or "Nobody I know ever wins!" Hopefully I can dispel the myths you've been confronted with in the past, as I talk you through the process of how I actually won a car. I am proof that it really can be achieved, with relatively little effort. Go for it – make your dreams come true!

Little did I know it at the time but the routine shopping trip to my local Safeway store, with two irritable young children in tow, was to be the start of a series of life-enhancing journeys for me, and a source of great pride to my family; I was about to win a car.

The excitement of discovery

On entering the store, we were greeted by a large 'WIN THIS CAR' sign attached to a gleaming metallic blue Nissan Micra that had somehow been squeezed through the entrance doors, and was waiting on display in the foyer. By the time the two boys had negotiated the trolley around several obstructions, and arrived in the store (without clipping too many people's ankles) I had acquired the entry instructions to the competition. I had that excited itchy feeling that the prize was already mine, and for once, I knew that today would be a great day. I experienced that inward joyful humming sensation (that thankfully nobody else can hear when it happens) as I busily gathered the groceries I required, and a ridiculous, infectious grin. My car was in the foyer, and all I had to do was find a way to get hold of the keys and registration document – no problem! I knew deep inside that the prize was already mine, mine, mine!

The challenge

So just what do you have to DO to win a car? You can expect it to be a little more involved than winning a trip to a theme park and for the qualifier to cost more than a tin of baked beans; this competition was no different. All I had to do was produce a £50 Safeway shopping receipt (which was time-restricted to the duration of the competition) and complete the sentence **"I would like to win a new Nissan Micra from Safeway because…"** How difficult could that be?

I wouldn't normally have spent £50 on my weekly food shopping, as I was on a very restricted budget whilst taking a career break, so I knew that I wouldn't be able to afford to submit many entries. The challenge was on! I had two weeks to enter as many times as possible, whilst spending more than I could really afford on shopping, just to obtain the shopping receipts. I even obtained an extra receipt from a friend, to support my good cause.

Motives for entering the competition

Without a clear motive fixing your drive (pardon the pun), there is very little chance of winning anything. So where did my enthusiasm stem from? I was determined to win this car for my mom, as a 'thank you' surprise gift following her generosity in buying my (then) current car for me. That was my focus. I visualized her joy at receiving the prize. That was my mom's car in the foyer – all I had to do was get it home for her!

Creating car-themed slogans

I decided to use one of my chances by adapting a 'classic' slogan that other people had won cars with in the past – maybe the manager hadn't heard the original version, and I'd win with very little effort (shame on me!). The other two would be entirely my own creations.

The first slogan was:

"…it's **supercontouredfuturisticextravaluespacious.**" This was based on a song from the *Mary Poppins* film.

Next, I listed everything that summed up Nissan, small cars, Safeway supermarkets, and shopping trips in general. This task took a couple of days. Finally, I had a list that could be used for cross-purposes. I based my second slogan on the 'nippiness' of the car and beating the British hobby of standing in queues. This slogan was: "…**It's the ultimate queue-buster.**" I wasn't sure that this slogan had winning potential, but was running short on time, so submitted it using my friend's receipt as the entry qualifier, rather like a bonus entry really.

For my third and final attempt, I decided to use a logical approach, and work on the psychology of winning – I knew that the manager had to detect my enthusiasm, in order to convince him to choose my entry as the overall winner. I was permitted to use up to ten words to complete the slogan, so I aimed to hyphenate my words, and use a rhyme.

Road rage versus trolley rage

I had it at last; my theme would be trolley rage versus road rage! I thought this was likely to be very different from any other entry, assuming that most people will not take time to enter a slogan competition, cannot make word associations, and have very poor rhyming skills.

I wrote out several versions of my slogan, incorporating different types of word-play; 'head-turning' and 'queue-hopping' could equally apply to a car and a person, as could the words 'geared up for', so I decided to incorporate these three ideas. Another consideration was the golden rule of always including the name of the sponsor and the product, so I had to include 'Safeway' and 'Nissan' to be hopeful of an outright win. There was only one prize on offer, so my final slogan had to be punchy and brilliant – something the judge had never come across before.

My third and final slogan was: '…Head-turning, queue-hopping, Nissan's geared for Safeway shopping'. I felt really good about this.

The prize promise

I had jokingly mentioned to my mom that she would have a nice new car by Monday morning (secretly willing it to be true); she just humored me, as usual. She didn't believe that real people ever won cars, always considering that the winners of expensive prizes were a 'fix', and that they would already have been selected before the competition started. I was itching to win it, even if it was just to prove her wrong!

Tensions and tumbles

Sunday night was a restless one for me – I couldn't sleep, because I had been mentally planning my acceptance speech. Monday morning was unbearable – I even had breakfast early, so that I would be ready for the congratulatory phone call to come through. I then sat down and waited, and waited… I even complained to my husband that I should have been contacted about my win by now – he just smirked, and went off to work as per normal, never really expecting me to have won it anyway.

At 10am the phone rang; it was the manager from Safeway, and yes, my dream had come true. The car was mine at last. I couldn't believe my luck, and phoned my parents immediately, and told my mom that there was a brand new car waiting for her to collect. Then my joy took an unexpected tumble; I had to re-order my thoughts and make rapid decisions… curiously, mom didn't want the car; she was pleased with the one she already possessed. The Micra was well and truly mine now – wow!

Collecting my car

I had just ten minutes to prepare myself, get changed and be at the Safeway store for a photo shoot and the presentation of my prize. Various scenarios had raced through my head as I drove to the store to meet the manager and members of the press. It was a huge event for me, and I was really nervous at the prospect of facing the media and driving my car out through the tight gap between the shop doors with everyone watching. What if I crashed it? My parents were already there in the foyer waiting for me – they were beaming with pride! Secretly, I hoped my mom would alter her decision about accepting my generous gift to her when she saw 'her new car', but she didn't, much to my immense surprise.

The car still had all of the 'WIN THIS CAR' stickers plastered all over it as we hit the streets whilst on a test drive. The whole town would now be my audience – it was a surreal experience. It certainly lived up to its reputation as a queue-hopper.

The chuckle factor

During the handover of the keys presentation, I asked the manager why he had picked my slogan as the winner. He said that out of the five hundred entries that he had received, only mine had made him chuckle.

Publicity

My presentation was just the start of the publicity process for the store, which is obviously highly important in all competitions of this type. My picture appeared in the local paper, and I took part in a local radio interview – these were both unusual, enjoyable experiences in their own right.

Tips and hints for winning a car

- There are very few entries for high value competitions – most people assume they have very little chance of winning these

- Keep your slogan short and witty

- Include the promoter's name and the product in at least one of your entries

- Try to use word-plays or puns

- Look out for the slogans that other people have previously won prizes with, and then adapt them for your purpose

- Mentioning a few engine parts will help

- List all words you associate with the theme before you attempt to write your slogan

- Obtain any qualifying receipts within the restrictive time limits (if applicable)

- Focus on your motives for winning the prize

The Value of Research

" Money won is twice as sweet as money earned. **"**

Paul Newman

Chapter 8
The Value of Research

Many of us will remember our teachers' advisory comments from our school days: "If you don't do your homework, you won't get good results." You will not be surprised to hear that this is the same for some competitions – if you fail to research a topic, you will lose out to somebody who has taken the time to do it. Here are a few tips that will guide you toward the prizes you could be on your way to winning.

Viewing the work of previous winners

One very useful benefit of the internet is that you can easily access many previous years' worth of winning entries to high profile competitions which require you to submit photographs or designs. The obvious advantage of this is that you are given a very clear indication of what the judging panel are actually seeking from an entrant, and the caliber of previous submissions. Armed with this valuable information, you will then be in an excellent, advantageous position which will enable you to tailor your photographic or art/design work to the competition themes that the promoter has requested. You will have a huge advantage over those entrants that do not do their research.

Check out the judge's website

Usually, the name of the person judging a competition will be mentioned on the entry form or on an information leaflet. It would be a sensible idea for you to perform a web search on the judge – he or she might have a web page that will give you an insight into what he or she finds important in a piece of relevant work. This could apply equally well to art, photographs, poems, creative writing, music or journalistic articles; the list is endless.

Current contests online

A selection of photographic submissions (or artwork) for a current competition might also be displayed on the website – study them carefully. If you are willing to have your work displayed in this manner, leave your entry until very close to the competition submission deadline, so that nobody steals your ideas (or your images) or uses them to their own advantage.

Copyright issues

Read the small print carefully; ensure that you are agreeing to retain copyright for your work once you have uploaded it onto the website. This applies to images and text documents. For written work, the author retains copyright, unless sold or transferred. In photography, copyright (unless sold or transferred) belongs to the person taking the photograph, not to the person whose image is represented in the photo itself. There will probably be a clause that allows for any prize-winning images to be licenced, free of charge, for publication at a later date. Check also whether or not there is a clause assigning the competition promoter the right to display all entries online (once online it is often difficult to get it removed).

PRIZE T!P

If you're hoping to win a car or holiday, I suggest you look up the latest design features of new models of cars, or some unique 'local' information relating to the holiday resort where your prize will be based (i.e. festivals, famous residents or traditions).

Requesting brochures from websites

If you have plenty of time left before the competition closing date, try contacting the company by email to request their promotional brochures (they do not need to know that it is related to their competition, and will probably be more helpful if they consider you to be a potential customer). This will give you a unique advantage over many other competitors, as you will be able to gain an insight in to any motives behind the competition, as well as getting a feel for any useful phrases and ideologies that are important to the company.

Customizing specific to a company

If this is a quiz or prize draw style contest, rather than one that requires a clever slogan submission, why not spruce up your entry in an attempt to impress the competition sponsors? Do this by cutting out any distinctive photographs from brochures that you have managed to obtain from the company and customize your postcards or envelopes with them. Flattery really does work.

Books – a wealth of reliable information

The internet, encyclopedias and promotional literature are valuable research tools that you cannot afford to pass up in your quest for the big value prizes. Bear in mind though, that reference books (in general) provide the most reliable facts and figures relating only to the year in which the book was published.

The accuracy of blogs and forums

The internet is constantly updated, but may not be entirely accurate in the detail it portrays. Use official sites for reference purposes, rather than blogs or forums, which might reveal information based upon opinion not fact. There is a wealth of instantly accessed information available to you – read a range of articles on the same subject; no two are likely to give the same detail.

PRIZE T!P
It is essential that your computer is adequately protected against incoming viruses when you are actively surfing the internet. Update your anti-virus software weekly if possible.

Search online for your slogan

If you are considering entering an off-the-shelf popular slogan in its unaltered form into a competition, then an excellent idea is to perform an internet search for it. Check if it has appeared before in a relevant competition, or whether a slightly different one has previously won a prize similar to the one you are hoping to win. If you find that the desired slogan does not score any hits or is not mentioned in relation to the company which is sponsoring or promoting the competition that you are planning to enter, then it is probably worth sending it in as one of your entries.

Search for winners

Checking out what your rivals have submitted for previous competitions is easier said than done. The best way is to log onto the promoter's website, and see whether or not there is a mention of any previous competitions. Also check for any clever advertising phrases that they are using; this is an indication of what the company is looking for in a prize-winning slogan.

PRIZE T!P

It is unusual for high value prize competitions not to have a question (or several questions) that require you to look up a few facts or to check the promoter's website. A little time spent researching this information will set you aside from the majority of casual compers who are unlikely to make the effort.

Coded information

There may be specific details for a competition that can only be found through the website, such as a 'code' which ensures that you have viewed the relevant marketing article or advertisement. The aim is also to encourage you to make a purchase whilst you browse the site.

Tips for researching a competition

- Use the internet (combined with an encyclopedia) to research quiz type qualifying questions that you are required to answer

- Research the promoters and the prize products prior to penning your slogan. Include product or location-specific information if possible, especially if you are entering to win a car or a holiday

- Previous winning photos or designs are often posted on manufacturers' websites – use these to gain ideas for your own entry

- Beware of internet competitions that request inappropriate personal data; if in doubt, don't enter

- You might need to access a website to release or check a prize code (usually found on packaging or magazines)

Keeping Records

66 Whoever said "It's not whether you win or lose that counts" probably lost. **99**

Mary Ashton Livermore

Chapter 9
Keeping Records

Being organized doesn't necessarily mean that you have to change your lifestyle. Keeping records of your wins and progress will bring you many hours of pleasure in the future; much like looking through treasured photos. There are many ideas listed in this section to choose from – select your favorites and make them a showpiece for your friends and family. A little time gloating over the big wins is always an ego boost.

A slogan notebook

A good measure of how your slogan-writing technique is improving is to list everything you have submitted to this style of competition in a diary or a notebook. Use one page per competition. At the top of the page write the closing date, the promoter's name and the winner's notification date (if it is mentioned in the small print details in the rules); this helps to focus your attention, and ensures you do not miss a deadline. List the slogans that you have submitted and also which prizes are on offer.

No contact

It is unlikely that you will be notified by the competition organizers unless you are a winner; in this case, you have a clear idea which slogans have not been successful for you.

Highlight your winners

Use a highlighter pen to identify each slogan in your record book that has won a prize for you, and add them to the list of your favorites. Remember – if these slogans have won once, they can do it again. Consider re-using them for a similar competition or theme of prize either 'as is' or with slight modifications. Milk your success as much as possible rather than wasting time and effort writing new slogans from scratch.

Spotting trends

Over a period of time you should see a trend developing as your confidence and originality intertwine. I occasionally look back at my original slogan book (I have several that I keep on my bookshelf). My original efforts were definitely of a much lower quality than those that I churn out now, and there is really no surprise that they did not win anything; on the whole, they were bland and uninteresting.

It gets easier

I realize now that I needed to inject a little humor, a pun or two, and bucket-loads of praise into my writing. I had nobody to guide me – it was purely trial and error on my part. I remember how difficult I found the process of writing slogans at that phase in my comping journey, and the hours that I spent on each one – it is far easier now for me and the results infinitely better. It is a big confidence boost to see just how much your time and effort has paid off in terms of quality.

Add up your earnings

Each time you win a prize, record its approximate value in a book or spreadsheet. I do this by listing the date, description and value of the prize in the file where I keep my other competition details. You might need this to fill in a tax return (see Chapter 1), but I do it for my own self-gratification. I like to assign a monetary equivalence to my success. I do not record anything until I have received the prize (a few do not arrive at all). At the end of the year I tally my winnings and start a new sheet. This will be an extra incentive to try even harder in the forthcoming year.

PRIZE T!P
ADVANCE NOTICE
Keeping records of your prize-winnings also gives you an indication of when the majority of competitions take place in your locality (good news for hunting down entry forms during the forthcoming year), and the type of competitions that you have been successful at. Target the same venues and suppliers in the future.

Potential gains

During some years, the total value of the prizes that I have won has been more than I have earned from full-time employment, even though I only enter competitions on a casual, ad hoc basis. The potential monetary and material gains of a career comper are absolutely colossal.

Scrap booking

The joy of reading of your own success never goes away. Keep all of your congratulatory letters, newspaper cuttings, event ticket stubs and photos together in one place. Keep thank you notes from your friends here too, as a reminder that your hobby is shared with the people that are special to you. A date-ordered scrap book is a wonderful idea for this.

Banish despondency

We all get despondent months when our winning spree takes a dip – it will happen, and there's not much you can do about it except to remain patient and keep trying. You must maintain your will to succeed; or you are setting yourself on the path to failure. I find that flicking through my scrapbook and gloating at my freebie acquisitions revives my enthusiasm and renews my vigor – often the photos make me chuckle as well.

" The winner's edge is not in a gifted birth, a high IQ, or in talent. The winner's edge is all in the attitude... **"**

Denis Waitley

Display and be proud

A few photos of your big wins could be displayed prominently in your study area at home or elsewhere where they can be seen easily. These are a great talking point for your visitors, especially if the photos contain a well-known celebrity, a beauty makeover, or a spectacular holiday setting.

PRIZE T!P

I retain the leaflets and newspaper promotions which advertise competitions until after the closing date. These are a useful memory trigger if you do win a prize that you don't remember entering for, or need to check the small print details in the rules section. Most winners will be notified within six to eight weeks of the competition closing date, so this is how long you need to keep the details for.

Exclusivity in poetry and short story competitions

In the case of poetry and short story competitions, once the winner-notification period has expired, you should be free to submit your work to another competition if you wish, since the rules often require exclusivity. You might be offered the opportunity to have your work returned to you if you enclose a stamped self-addressed envelope.

Index